TOTALLY FREE BEST PRIVATE HOSPITALS IN INDIA

(ALMOST FREE INCLUDING FOOD & ACCOMMODATION)

PRADIP KUMAR RAY

<u>Dedication</u>

My only son Shri Pragyan Ray and wife Sonali Roy, close relatives and future generations of me and relatives and of course the needy patient of my country.

Pradip Kumar Ray, Burdwan.

<u>Disclaimer</u>

The contents of this book are meant merely for information purposes. The information contained herein is subject to updating, completion, revision, verification, and amendment. The information provided herein is not intended for distribution to, or use by, any person in any jurisdiction where such distribution or use would (by reason of that person's nationality, residence or otherwise) be contrary to law or regulation.

All information including news articles published in this book is strictly for general information purpose only. It does not provide any warranty about the authenticity and accuracy of such information. It will not be held responsible for any loss and/or damage that arise or is incurred by the use of such information. Rates and offers as may be applicable at the time of applying for a product may vary from that mentioned above.

Pradip Kumar Ray

Contents

Foreword

<u>**My word**</u>

The aim of this book is to focus on information and basic guide of free and low cost best private hospitals in India. The author's aim to provide information to the citizens in India about affordable health and wellness as well as specialist services through the best private hospitals at free of cost or at low cost in India will be helpful to needy patients.. In such a situation, the author's enquiry, the curiosity to know the unknown and raise awareness by combining the explanations of different scopes of health care with low cost and free of cost at best private hospitals will be successful by reading this book.

Babli Roy. (Manuscript Reader)

Preface

My word

The aim of this book is to focus on information and basic guidelines for free and low-cost best private hospitals in India. The Indian public health sector encompasses 18% of total outpatient care and 44% of total inpatient care. Middle and upper-class individuals living in India tend to use public healthcare less than those with a lower standard of living. My aim is to provide information to the citizens in India about affordable health and wellness as well as specialist services through the best private hospitals free of cost or at low cost in India. In such a situation, my inquiry, the curiosity to know the unknown and raise awareness by combining the explanations of different scopes of health care with low cost and free of cost at best private hospitals will be successful by reading this book. This book will be a companion to all those who are seeking the best private hospitals at almost no cost including food and accommodation. This is my hope and I am confirmed about the fact that this book will help people to get the best specialist services in healthcare at absolutely no cost at the best private hospitals with the best doctors in India. So, I have enumerated here the top private hospitals of India with all the best medical facilities free of cost or low cost, including food and accommodation.

Pradip Kumar Ray, 223-A.B.Mukherjee Road, Nutanganj, Dighirpool, Bardhhaman – 713102.

Acknowledgements

<u>My gratitude and acknowledgment</u>
To complete this book I have taken help from various books, magazines, websites, social media such as Facebook, You-Tube, Quora, discussions with different patients and travellers and their various opinions, Wikipedia etc. My sincere gratitude to all of them and to the publisher of this book. These will help to increase the practical knowledge of the reader.

Pradip Kumar Ray.

Prologue

Author Introduction

The author decided to voluntarily retire from banking services after 31+ years of service. At that time, he was posted as Chief Manager (Offing) in the Purshura branch of SBI. At SBI, he worked in various activities like Branch Manager, HR Manager, Systems Manager, etc. At that time, the hobby of the writer was to invent different magic and write different articles. His first book "Prerana" was published in 2013. His various articles and essays have already been published in a number of widely circulated and under-published newspapers and magazines. In the case of magic, biodata with the author's image was published in the World Directory of Magicians.

The educational qualifications of the author are B.Sc. (Hons. in Physics), M.Sc. (Computer Science), Computer Application Post Graduate Diploma (PGDCA), Cisco Certified Network Associates-Global (CCNA), Certified Associate of the Indian Institute of Banking (CAIIB). He has also done various certificate courses such as photo, video, and audio editing, animation, hardware, COBOL programming, Hindi Pragya courses, etc.

After retiring, the author also worked with several academies as an expert instructor in "Banking" and now works on his YouTube channel, Facebook page, Website, Blog, Stock Photography, various articles, self-published books, etc., and he is also engaged in internet-based work.

The following Books which are written by Author have already been published and available on Amazon, Flip cart, Notion Press, and Pothi's Online Outlet.

In Bengali:- 1) Prerana 2) Anuprerana 3) Mahabharate Ki Ki Tathya Chitrita Achhe Ja Ajo Prasangik? 4) Puran Kahineer Antarnihita Artha 5) Ramayaner Ajana Tathya 6) Manabatar Pujari Swalpa Prichita Bharatiyer Kahinee. 7) Ashepasher Gachh Gachhalir Soundarya O Oshadhi Gun. 8) Jana Manusher Ajana Kahinee 9) Baba Mane- Maa Mane-- 10) Kalpanay, Kheyalr O Kathane Corona 11) Nijer Madhyei Nije

In English:- 1) How to Write Banking Letter (For Banker & Customer) More than 120 Relevant sample letters. 2) How to write an email (ethics, examples & samples of emails). 3) The story of a little-known Indian worshiper of humanity. 4) Secrets of Motivation & Inspiration. 5) Unpopular but Attracting with Historical Interest Tourist Place in

Bardhhaman. 6) Digital Banking Ready Reference for Customer. 7) 'Corona' in Imagination, Troll & Mimes. 8) MCQ with Answers for BC & BF Examination 9) How to Improve Your Mental Strength 10) Short Stories and Tales 11)GENERAL APTITUDE (CSIR Net-Previous Q & A with explanation and hint to solve)

In Hindi: - 1) Prerak Koushal Me Sudhar Kaise Kare. 2) Chhatra Aour Bankaro Ke Lie Banking. 3) "Corona" - Kathan, Troll & Mimes. 4) Oitihasik Akarshak Parjatan Sthal, Burdwan 5) Apni Manasik Shakti Ka Bikash Kaise Kre 6) Sambandha Bipanan Shikhne Ka Sabse Achchha Tarika

Publisher.

Prologue

The creation of this book was inspired by the interest and inspiration of countless readers of my published book and the followers and viewers of my blog, website, Facebook page, YouTube, etc.

Website–https://pkrbur.com; www.rayfamily.itgo.com

Blog- Motivational in Bengali- https://pkrnet.blogspot.com;

Blog- Motivational in Hindi – https://pkrhindi.blogspot.com

Blog – Motivational in English- https://pkrbur.com/blog-motivational/

Blog – Tour and Travel - https://pkrbur.com/blog-tour-travel/

Blog – Banking for Students – https://pkrbank.blogspot.com

Blog–Banking Technology for Customers–https://pkrbur.com/blog-banking-technology-for-customer/

PKR Video & Audio - https://pkrbur.com/p-k-r-video-audio-links/

FACEBOOK PAGE - https://www.facebook.com/pradip1/

FACEBOOK GROUP:-Motivational &Inspirational https://www.facebook.com/groups/Motivation62

FACEBOOK - https://www.facebook.com/profile.php?id=100009528403607

YouTube-SHANTANURUDRA-Disguise name of Pradip Kr. Ray –https://www.youtube.com/channel/UC9ZCD6070OMsP0pdwcgSBgwY

YouTube - PRADIP KUMAR RAY -PKRNET, BURDWAN

https://www.youtube.com/channel/UC5wyD8s3usaRfMDduEjR1LQ?view_as=subscriber

E-Mail:pradip.ray1911@gmail.com, Pkrnet.burdwan@gmail.com

To See Author's Published Books, Go to the link: https://pkrbur.com/professional/

Sai baba hospital Whitefield, Bangalore(Totally Free)

Sri Sathya Sai Institute of Higher Medical Sciences
EPIP Area, Whitefield,
Bangalore 560 066,
Karnataka, INDIA.
Help Desk: +91-80 4710 4600
Mobile: +91-8296004600
(080)-28004600 / 28411500
Call +91-80-4710-4600 for appointments between 8 AM to 4 PM on
weekdays

This hospital provides patient care facilities to all casts, classes, creeds, gender, religion, or nationality. It is one of the largest super specialty hospitals in the world; this hospital provides many medical facilities totally free of charge absolutely. I am talking about these of the Saibaba hospital Whitefield, Bangalore, India. The Sri Sathya Sai Institute of Higher Medical Science is also popularly known as a super specialty hospital for territorial health care.

The Hospital is situated in the heart of white field Bangalore. This hospital was established by Sri Sathya sai baba on 19th January 2001. This hospital provides all kinds of facilities to all kinds of people, it may be any caste class creed gender religion or nationality. More importantly, all the facilities are totally free of cost which is the most important part of this hospital.

You must understand that there is no cash counter in this hospital. You need to know what the super-specialty hospital offers. Here you go for cardiology, cardiothoracic and vascular surgery then neurology and neurosurgery, and radiology. This hospital also has a laboratory that is of a high standard and very hygienic all the way such as pathology, microbiology, biochemistry labs, blood bank, and many more things that help all kinds of patients.

Physiotherapy, dietary, and counseling are also provided in this hospital. This hospital is popularly known as the temple of healing and these are all the words suggested by or given by the patient who was treated here. It has the state of the art of technology and high quality.

Kindly note that the Hospital does not have a billing counter. It has the first come first serve policy; don't pay anything to any staff. The patient who seeks treatment can send the medical report by email. Visiting hours in the hospital are from 4 to 6 p.m.

Now I will guide you to where this hospital is located. All of you must know that Bangalore is the IT hub in the entire world. This hospital is in the IT hub of Whitefield.

Now I will guide you on how to reach this hospital and how you will reach Bangalore from a different destination. Bangalore has a very good facility for buses and there is a popular area called majestic in Bangalore. If you get down in a Bangalore from any town or any city or any from the majestic you have the passes okay that is number 3 3 5 a and 3 3 5 e from the market that is a care market you have 3 3 5 or 3 3 5 B and 3 3. If I see, if you are traveling from the Train and you are trying to reach white field from the train you have to get down at hoody and reach.

<u>Hospital Overview:</u>

It is a 333-bedded tertiary care hospital inaugurated by the then Prime Minister of India, Sri Atal Behari Vajpayee; it is located in the picturesque suburbs of Whitefield in the garden city of Bangalore, Karnataka, India. Shaped in the form of the letter K, the Hospital stands for Karuna or compassion and has been successful in healing thousands of diseased hearts and brains and returning to the society a healthy and grateful individual touched by the spirit of sacrifice and transformed to make a difference to the fellow human beings.

Sri Sathya Sai Institute of Higher Medical Sciences is equipped with state-of-art diagnostic and treatment facilities, highly skilled medical, nursing, and paramedical professionals delivering care with love and compassion, in a clean, aesthetic and spiritual environment ensuring that healing happens in the body, mind, and spirit.

Infrastructure-wise, Hospital has state of an art 1.5 Tesla Siemens Magnetom Area MRI Scanner, 128 slice HD 750 GE CT Scanner, Siemens Artis Zee Biplane CathLab, Philips Monoplane Cathlab, Medtronic S7 Neuro-navigation system, 8 fully equipped operation theaters, automated biochemistry and microbiology analyzers, high-end diagnostic Cardiology equipment, full-blown Hospital Information System eHIS from Computer Science Corporation and Fuji Synapse PACS system.

Apart from patient care, Hospital is also active in creating the next generation of doctors, nurses, and technologists. Hospital has a very active postgraduate and post-doctoral program affiliated with the National Board of Examinations providing DNB in Cardiac Surgery, Neurosurgery, Cardiology, Anaesthesiology, and Radiology. Additionally Hospital also has post-doctoral fellowships in Interventional Cardiology, Cardiac Anaesthesia, Critical Care Anaesthesia, and Cross-sectional imaging. In the paramedical field, Hospital provides BSc Nursing, BSc Imaging Technology, BSc Perfusion Technology, BSc Anaesthesia Technology, BSc Cardiac Technology, and BSc Medical Laboratory Technology.

Sri Sathya Sai Central Trust, Prasanthi Nilayam is perhaps the only charitable trust in INDIA to offer complete medical care including consultation, diagnosis, comprehensive treatment and follow – up and diet at the primary, secondary and tertiary levels to all patients free of all charges irrespective of his caste, creed, religion or economic status.

<u>APPOINTMENTS</u>

Welcome to Sri Sathya Sai Institute of Higher Medical Sciences, Whitefield. This hospital is a tertiary care institution that caters to the specialties of Cardiology, Cardiothoracic, and vascular surgery, Neurology, and Neurosurgery.

The following information is a general guide for patients who would like to avail the of free medical care at Sri Sathya Sai Institute of Higher Medical Sciences, Whitefield.

Please note the following:

1. All medical service provided to patients of SSSIHMS Whitefield is totally free of charge.
2. The hospital does not have a billing counter.
3. The hospital strictly conforms to a first come first serve policy with provisions for emergency medical conditions.
4. Patients and patient attendees are advised not to pay anyone who claims to be a staff member of SSSIHMS Whitefield, for any service whatsoever. Immediately bring such individuals to the notice of the Hospital Security.
5. Patients seeking treatment here can call the Hospital Helpline number 080-47104600 for getting an appointment for an OPD consultation at the Hospital.
6. Due to the current COVID situation, for the safety of patients and staff, the hospital is requiring patients to come with negative RT PCR report.

<u>Visiting Hours:</u>

- The general visiting hours are from 4:00 PM to 6:00 PM.
- When outside visitors wish to see a patient, the attendant staying with the patient may approach the Security at the gate I, leave his/her attendant pass with him, collect the Visitors' pass from Security, and proceed to the wards.
- After visiting the patients, the attendant can collect his/her pass after seeing off the visitors.

<u>In-patient Attendants:</u>

- For every in-patient, one attendant has to remain on campus. He/she will be given the attendant pass by the respective ward sister.
- In the Neuro ward, during the rounds by the consultants and doctors, the patient attendants are expected to be around.
- Additional attendants are allowed only if the patients are immobile, have any disability, and need assistance for moving around or in any other case, as opined by the concerned doctor.
- Only under instructions from a doctor is an additional attendant pass issued.

<u>OUTPATIENT CONSULTATION</u>

<u>Registration</u>

Please bring all your previous medical records. Please bring a valid proof of address. The following proofs are accepted. Aadhar Card (preferred), Ration card, Voters id, Driver's license, Passport – this is compulsory for all foreign nationals. One attendant is compulsory. You will first be screened to be a patient of either of the specialties offered by SSIHMS and only then registered.

<u>Appointment</u>

The patient is required to call the patient help desk at 080-47104600 to get an appointment. Then will get an SMS with the appointment date and timing.

Gate No.2

At Gate No.2, you will need to send show the appointment SMS to the security. You may then proceed to the Screening / Reception block.

Screening / Reception block

Here you will be directed to the appropriate section – cardiac or neuro. The doctors will evaluate your condition and advise you accordingly. Once advised by the doctors in the screening block to approach the OPD, you may proceed to the appropriate OPD.

Out-Patient Department

As you enter the main hall of the hospital, the Cardiac OPD is to your left-hand side and the Neuro OPD is across the hall on your right-hand side. There will be volunteers at the entrance to guide you to the appropriate OPD.

<u>Follow-up/ Revisit Patients</u>

i. Come to the hospital only if you have been specifically advised to do so in your discharge summary.

v. To avoid any eventualities, please check the **date** of your revisit on your discharge summary and make sure you come on that date.

v. If any complications arise, for any reason you would like to visit the hospital please call the hospital and confirm whether it is absolutely necessary for you to travel to the hospital.

v. Patient Help Desk – 080-47104600

<u>INPATIENT ADMISSIONS</u>

Due to the current COVID pandemic, RT PCR is mandatory for admission for both patients and attendants for admission. On the date of admission, you will be completely screened by the doctors. You will be admitted only after you are found fit for surgery. One attendant is compulsory. Bring all previous medical records. Both, records from other medical institutions and any medical records given to you by SSSIHMS. To avoid any inconvenience, make your travel arrangements such that you come to the hospital on the appointed day, before 8.30 a.m.

<u>Telemedicine</u>

The department of telemedicine, SSSIHMS, Whitefield is part of the Sri Sathya Sai Telehealth Network that includes both the sister institutions at Prasanthigram and Whitefield.

<u>Nodal point Location</u>

<u>In West Bengal – Barrackpore</u>

Sri Sathya Sai Seva Kendra,
1, Riverside Road (Beside Mangal Pandey Park),
Barrackpore Cantonment, Barrackpore, North 24 Paraganas,
Pin – 700120. West Bengal.
Telephone: 033- 25450329
Email: telemedbkp@gmail.com
In Orissa – Bhubaneswar
Sri Sathya Sai Seva Samiti, Unit III, Kharavel Nagar, (Opp. Nalini Devi Womens' College of Teacher Education), Bhubaneswar, Odisha, Pin: 769 010, Phone: 0674-2391090, 8895268090
Email: telemedbbsr@gmail.com

Sri Sathya Sai Telehealth Network offers consultation in Neuro and Cardiac post-operative care for patients operated on at SSSIHMS. Patients who are diagnosed with such ailments, who have already consulted a doctor and have previous medical records (reports/ scans) readily available, may approach the nodal center.

FACILITIES

Welcome to Sri Sathya Sai Institute of Higher Medical Sciences, Whitefield. This hospital is a tertiary care institution that caters to the specialties of Cardiology, Cardiothoracic, and vascular surgery, Neurology, and Neurosurgery. Given below is general information about various facilities in and around the Hospital.

HOW TO REACH

The Hospital is around 40 km from the Bangalore International Airport, 10 km from HAL airport, and 24 km from the Railway & Bus station of the city: Kempegowda bus station, locally called 'Majestic bus stop'. Taxicab services are available from both the airport and the railway station. Prepaid auto rickshaw service is available at the railway station. The following Public Transport Bus routes are available:

- Volvo air-conditioned public transport service "BIAS" (Bangalore International Airport Service) is available from the Airport to Sri Sathya Sai Baba Ashram, Kadugodi. SSSIHMS is 5 kilometers from Kadugodi – by public transport/taxi / auto-rickshaw.

- Volvo A/c and regular public transport services are available to and from KempeGowda Bus Stop

From Kempe Gowda Bus Stop towards SSSIHMS
Route No. Destination Platform No.
304 J Channasandra/ITPL 17
326 E Hosakote/ Hope Farm 17
319 C Kadugodi/ Hope Farm 17
334 J Kadugodi/Hope Farm 17
304 H Hope Farm / ITPL 17
319 F SSSIHMS 17
333 E Whitefield Rly. Stn/ Hope Farm 17
333H Kadugodi/ Hope Farm 17
109 Whitefield Rly. Stn./ Hope Farm 17
335H Kadugodi 17

Cantonment Railway station is another hub in Bangalore city which is very close to Shivajinagar Bus station. Passengers alighting from trains coming via this railway station may utilize the following route numbers.

From Shivaji Nagar towards SSSIHMS
Route No. Destination Platform No.
331 Brindavan/ITPL or Hope Farm B3
331E Belthur/Hope Farm A1
301 Channasandra/ Hope Farm D3
Depending on the bus route taken:

1. One may alight right in front of SSSIHMS. (335H)
2. One may alight at Pattandura Agrahara/ITPL and reach SSSIHMS after a 10-minute walk or by auto-rickshaw.
3. One alighting at Hope Farm may take a bus to ITPL/Pattandura Agrahara and either walk to SSSIHMS or use an auto-rickshaw.

<u>FOOD COURT</u>

Hospital has a low-cost canteen service for doctors, staff, students, and patients, patient attendants on campus which is run by Sri Sathya Sai Institute of Higher Medical Sciences, Whitefield, and Welfare Society. The Welfare Society also runs a bakery service for benefit of staff and patients.

Canteen coupons are available at the coupon counter, opened during the canteen serving hours. In-patient attendants are encouraged to purchase coupons in bulk to avoid crowding the coupon counter during peak hours. The breakfast counter closes by 9 AM, after which breakfast is served in the Bakery.

Canteen Timings:

Breakfast: 7:30 AM – 9:00 AM (in General Canteen)

Lunch: 12:30 PM to 2:00 PM

Afternoon Tea/Snacks: 4:00 PM to 5:30 PM

Dinner: 7:30 PM to 8:30 PM

Bakery Timings:

9:30 AM – 12:30 PM

2:30 PM – 9:00 PM

All items are sold at MRP.

All purchases have to be made in cash. Canteen coupons are not valid in the bakery.

Apart from this, there are several other eating options available outside the Hospital.

Food Court in orbit Mall has many eateries.

Hyderabad Cuisine:

After Manthra Restaurant, Brookfield, 11:00-4:00 and 6:30-11:00 / Ph no: 9986341029 / 080-41162811 /080-41162611 / Veg non veg.

Annapurna, Bengali cuisine

Before Big Bazaar, After SSSIHMS / 7.00 a.m to 10 p.m / Veg non veg.

Big Bazaar:

Beside ITPL / 11.00 a.m to 11.00 p.m

Booming Bakery & Sweets:

Before Big Bazaar, After SSSIHMS, 6.00 a.m to 10:30 p.m.

Cauvery bakery:

Aviva Junction / 5.00 AM to 10.00 p.m

Fruit Mandi:

After Manthra Restaurant, Brookfield

Hotel Hansika, Andhra Style:

Before BigBazar, After SSSIHMS / 12:00 – 10:30 / Veg non veg.

Hotel Sri Manjunatha:

Before BigBazar, After SSSIHMS / 7a.m to 10:30 p.m.

Lulu bakery:

Before Big Bazaar, After SSSIHMS / 6.00 a.m to 11:30 p.m.

Manjunatha Hotel:

Aviva Junction / 7.00 a.m to 10 p.m / Ph no 41693252

Manthra Restaurant:
After Cosmopolitan Mall
Milk Booth:
After Manthra Restaurant, Brookfield
Mini Bakery:
Near Andhra Spice / After Cosmopolitan Mall
Muthappan Bakery:
Aviva Junction
Nandini Andhra Style:
After Manthra Restaurant, Brookfield / 11:30-4:00 and 7:00-10:30 Veg non Veg
R.K. Fast Food:
Lane in front of SSSIHMS, Near Bus Depot / 6:30 a.m to 9:30 p.m Vegetarian
Rasam's Andhra Cuisine:
Whitefield / 12:00a.m – 3:00 p.m and 7:00 p.m -10:00 p.m / Ph no: 080-64552602
Shiv Sagar:
In Front of ITPL / 7.00 a.m to 10.00 p.m / Vegetarian
Sri Krishna Bakery:
In Front of ITPL / 6.00 a.m to 10.00 p.m
Sri Sathya Sai Bakery:
Aviva Junction / 6.00 a.m to 10.00 p.m / Ph no: 080-41142129
Only One:
Kundalahalli village / 12:30 p.m to 11:00 p.m / Ph No: 080-64542211, 080-64543311

<u>ACCOMMODATION</u>

Sai Salarpuria Dormitory is a low-cost dormitory facility for patient attendants of admitted patients.

1. The male/female attendants of the patients admitted to the Hospital are permitted to stay in the Salarpuria Block on payment of Rs.20/- per day.
2. The receipt for the Salarpuria block can be collected after paying the money in the Administration block **between 2:00 PM and 4:00 PM.**
3. Attendants who are unable to collect the receipt can pay the money to the In-charge of the Salarpuria block. This has to be regularized on the next working day.
4. Mat and blanket are provided to all the patient attendants in the Salarpuria block.

5. The date on the receipt includes a night's stay.
6. Apart from the stay patient attendants are advised not to pay money under any other circumstances (especially during festivals).
7. Dhobi facility is arranged in the Salarpuria Block on a payment basis.
8. Patients have to show the admission slip before paying for their stay as this facility is provided only for the relatives of the inpatients.
9. Relatives can relieve one another and the pass can be exchanged.

<u>CLOAKROOM</u>

Timings: 7:30 AM to 7:30 PM.

Patient attendants are advised not to keep any valuables in the cloakroom. In-patients and their attendants can also keep their luggage in the Salarpuria Block.

The Administration is not responsible for any loss from the cloakroom or the attendant's hostel.

<u>RAILWAY CONCESSION</u>

- Travel concession is provided at the time of discharge to only those patients who undergo cardiac surgery and interventional cardiac catheterization.
- Details of this procedure can be obtained from Sister in charge at Coronary Care Unit (CCU).
- Patients who undergo neurosurgery (for cancerous brain tumors only) are eligible for travel concession.

<u>PROHIBITED ITEMS FOR ENTRY</u>

   I. Cigarettes, Beedi, or any other smoking items
  II. Match Box, Cigarette lighter, or any other fire-producing items
 III. Tobacco, Pan Parag, Gutka, or any other littering items
 IV. Alcoholic Drinks
  V. Knife, Scissors
 VI. Inflammable materials
VII. Non-Vegetarian food items
VIII. Outside Food except for children

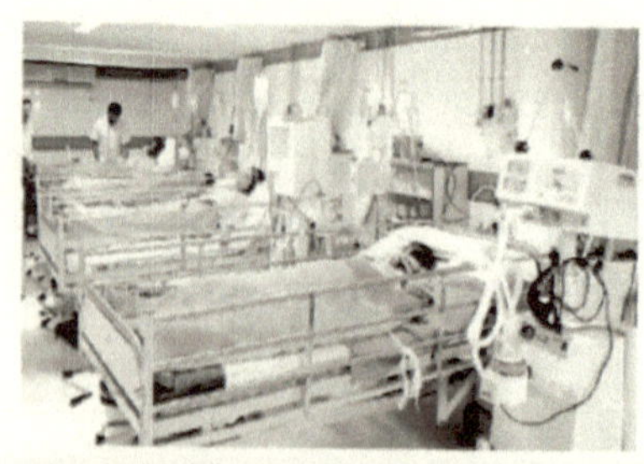
Provides patient care facilities
TO ALL
CASTE,
CLASS,
CREED,
GENDER,
RELIGION
NATIONALITY
There is no cash counter
TOTALLY FREE OF CHARGE

SUPER SPECIALITY
HOSPITAL OFFERS
FREE CARE FOR

CARDIOLOGY

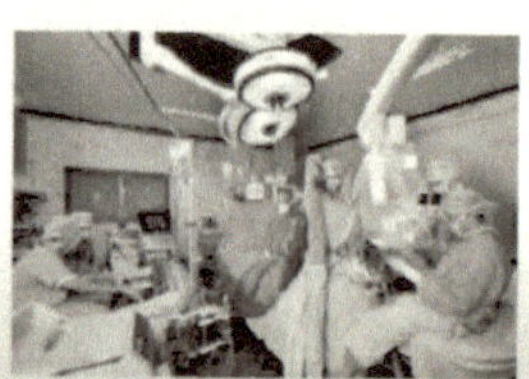

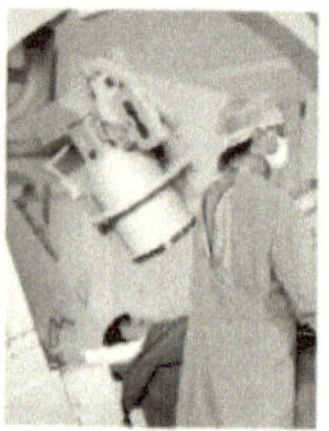

CARDIO THORACIC & VASCULAR SURGERY

RADIOLOGY

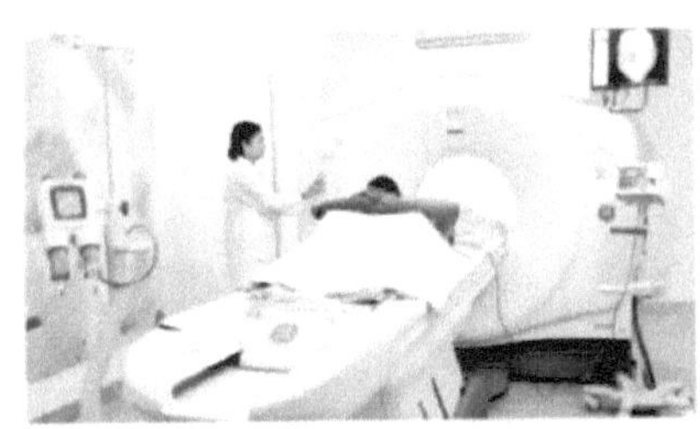

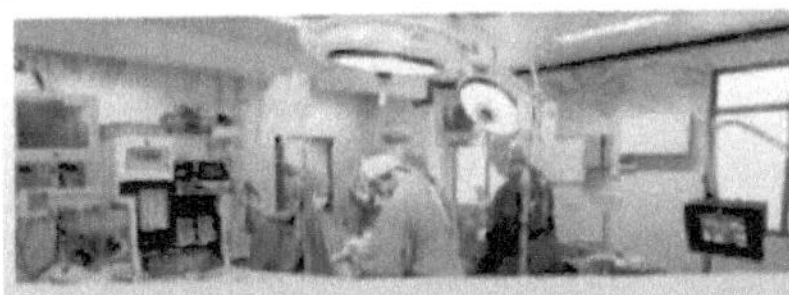

NEUROLOGY AND NEUROSURGERY

HOSPITAL ALSO HAS LABORATORY

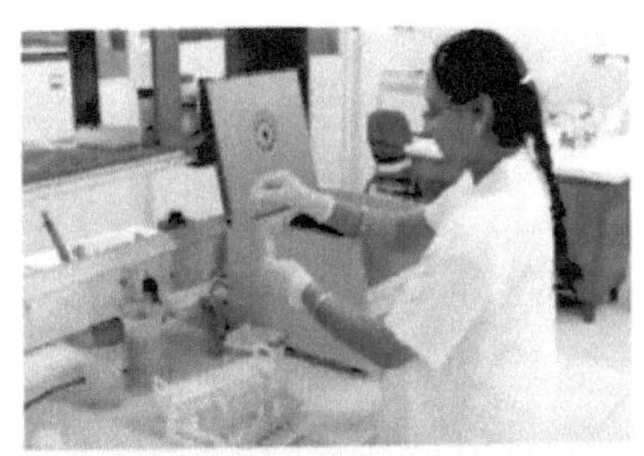

PATHOLOGY,
MICROBIOLOGY,
BIOCHEMISTRY LABS,
BLOOD BANK

PHYSIOTHERAPY, DIETARY
AND COUNSELING

'TEMPLE OF HEALING'

STATE- OF - THE - ART TECHNOLOGY
& HIGH QUALITY SERVICE

PATIENTS SPEAK

"NEW VISION, NEW LIFE"

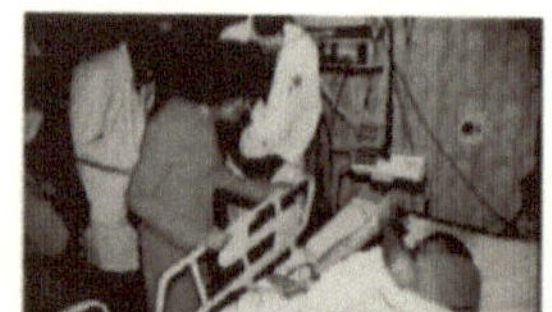

HE STEALS "HEARTS
WHILE HIS HEART HEALS"

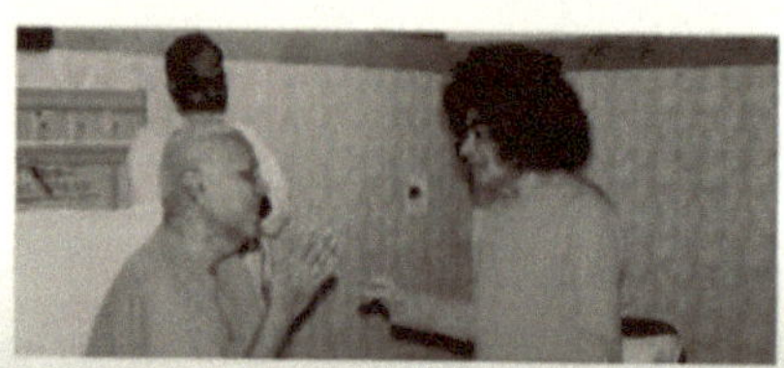

"FROM HEARTBREAK TO HAPPINESS"

PLEASE NOTE THE FOLLOWING

ALL MEDICAL SERVICE ARE FREE OF CHARGE
HOSPITAL DOES NOT HAVE A BILLING COUNTER
FIRST COME FIRST SERVE POLICY
DON'T PAY TO ANY STAFF
PATIENTS SEEKING TREATMENT CAN SEND
  MEDICAL REPORTS BY E-MAIL

VISITING HOURS
FROM 4:00 PM TO 6:00 PM

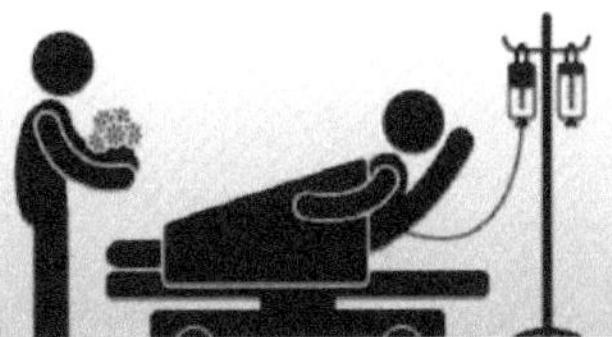

ADDRESS

SRI SATHYA SAI HOSPITAL
EPIP AREA, WHITEFIELD,
BANGALORE 560 066

80-28004600/28411500

adminblr@sssihms.org.in

BUS & TRAIN DETAILS

FROM MAJESTIC

335A & 335E

FROM K R MARKE

335, 335B, & 335C

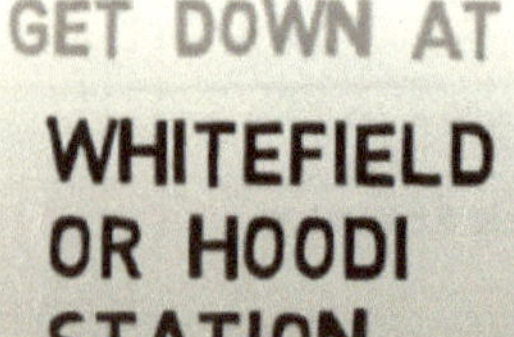

CHAPTER TWO

Satya Sai Sanjibani Hospital, Raipur, Chattisgarh(Totally Free)

(People whose age is less than 10 years – Free Treatment)
Helpdesk Number: **8010119000**

With over 2,40,000 children born every year with heart disease, a leading cause of Infant Mortality in India, its care remains grossly inadequate and beyond the reach of many. Trust has now embarked on a journey towards addressing the global burden of Congenital Heart Diseases through the **Sri Sathya Sai Sanjeevani Centre for Child Heart Care.**

The chain of Hospitals treats children Totally Free of Cost restoring dignity to a child's life and gifting a healthy childhood for them.

Sri Sathya Sai Sanjeevani began this journey by establishing the first dedicated **Totally Free of Cost** Centre for Child Heart Care at Atal Nagar (prev. Naya Raipur), Chhattisgarh in November 2012.

Chain of Hospitals rendering **Totally Free of Cost Pediatric Cardiac Care** focusing on Congenital Heart Disease irrespective of caste, creed, religion, nationality, and financial status.

<u>HOSPITAL SERVICES</u>

1. PEDIATRIC CARDIOLOGY 2. PEDIATRIC CARDIAC SURGERY 3. PEDIATRIC INTENSIVE CARE

<u>Diagnostics</u>
ECHO, ECG, X-Ray, Foetal Echocardiography, Diagnostic Angiography, Medical Management.

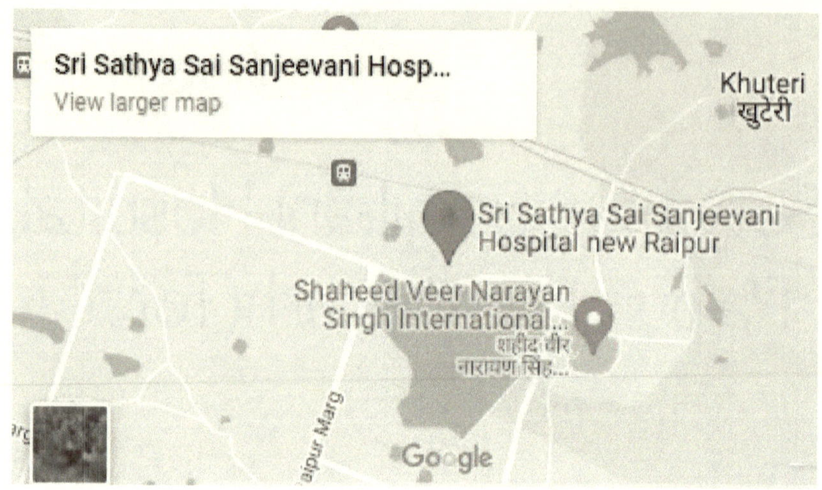

<u>Cath Interventions</u>

PDA device closure, ASD device closure, Balloon dilations, VSD device closure, EP Study, RF Ablations of SVTs.

<u>Surgical Spectrum</u>

Ventricular Septal Defect Closure, Inter Cardiac Repair, Atrial Septal Defect Closure, PDA Ligation, TAPVC Repair, Bidirectional Glenn shunt Stage, Mitral Valve Replacement, AV Canal Repair, Coarctation of Aorta, Warden's Procedure, VSD+A.O.Valve Repair, Arterial Switch Operation, Sam Excision, Double Valve Replacement, DCRV Repair, AP Window Closing, Coarctation of Aorta + PDA, Mitral Valve Repair Truncus Repair, Aortic Valve Replacement, Open Pulmonary Valvotomy, Senning's Repair, Total cavopulmonary connection, ALCAPA Repair, Arterial Switch Op + VSD Closure, Rastelli-s Procedure, PA Banding, Fontan / Kreutzer Procedure Stage, TRANS PA, RA Repair, Sinus Venosus Defect Repair, Brock's Procedure, Kawashima Repair, Schumacker's Repair, Ebstein's Anomalous, Broms Procedure, etc.

<u>Critical Care</u>

Over 50-bedded ICU (Combined), ECMO units, Isolation Rooms and Quarantine Areas and Zones, Over 65-bedded Step-Down and PACUs (Combined).

Patient Registration:

- **ATAL NAGAR:** Monday – Friday: Before 8 AM

Foetal ECHO at Atal Nagar: Saturday 10 AM to 12 PM, with prior appointment.CLOSED on Sundays & Public Holidays

Accompanying patients

Two(2) attendants will be allowed to accompany patients below 12 years of age and Only one (1) attendant will be allowed to accompany patients above 12 years

Documents

For registration, Please carry a government photo ID: Aadhar / PAN card of father/mother/guardian, Ration card, and Birth certificate of the child.

After registration, you will be issued a unique patient ID card which needs to be carried for any future visits to the hospital. After outpatient consultation, the medical team will advise you about any further treatment. Reports will be provided after consultation.

Canteen & accommodation

Food & Accommodation will be provided free of cost after admission for surgery/intervention. Outpatients and attendants may avail of canteen services.

Please note there is no appointment over the phone or by mail.

Canteen Services

- Lunch and Dinner shall be made available for attendants totally free of cost after admission
- Attendants are requested to follow medical advice with respect to pre-surgery/intervention medication, pre-operative care, surgery/intervention date, and post-operation/intervention care.
- Patients are particularly requested to be prepared to stay in the Hospital during a varying pre-operative waiting periods when the patient is observed by the medical team, before the actual surgery.
- Attendants should not change without prior permission.

<u>SPECIAL INSTRUCTIONS</u>

The hospital is closed on Sundays and public holidays. Usage of alcohol, gutkha, cigarette/bidi, and Pan Masala on the hospital premises will not be tolerated. Usage of mobile phones on the hospital premises is not allowed. All patient attendants are required to wear the ID tag given to them throughout their stay. It has three centers, in Atal Nagar, Chhattisgarh,

Palwal, Haryana, and Navi Mumbai, Maharashtra. The hospital is closed on Sundays and Public Holidays.

For registration, please carry government photo ID: 1a. Aadhar / PAN card of father/mother/guardian,

b. Ration card,c. Birth certificate of the child.

After registration, you will be issued a unique patient ID card upon which you will need to bring for any future visits to the hospital.

When the child is fit for travel, please bring the child to the hospital for Outpatient Consultation. After which, the medical team will provide you with a medical report and advice you about further treatment for the child.

All services at Sri Sathya Sai Sanjeevani are rendered totally free of cost, irrespective of caste, creed, nationality, religion, or financial status.

Sri Sathya Sai Sanjeevani specializes in Congenital Heart Disease ONLY. Patients of all ages with Congenital Heart Disease are welcome to visit the hospital.

Accommodation and food are provided free of cost to patients and attendants AFTER admission. Prior to admission, patients and attendants can avail the food services available in the Canteen.

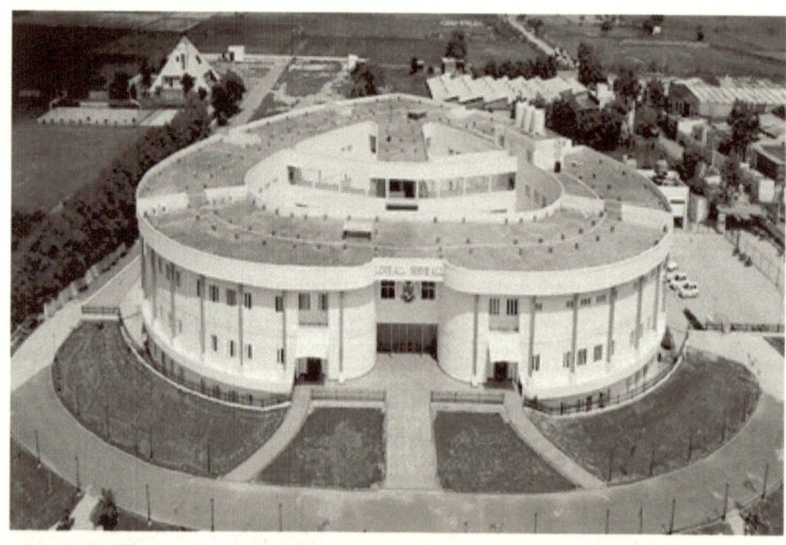

Outpatient Registration begins before 8 AM, Monday to Friday (Atal Nagar) and Monday to Saturday (Palwal).

Please visit the hospital for Outpatient Consultation (only when the patient is fit to travel), after which the medical team will provide you with a medical report and advice you on the treatment plan. Given the large number of children awaiting treatment in the country, the treatment of your child is subject to evaluation by the medical team. Please follow the advice given in your child's medical report. If you need further clarification, feel free to contact the hospital helpline numbers or email address. Two (2) attendants will be allowed to accompany patients below 12 years of age. Only one (1) attendant will be allowed to accompany patients above 12 years.

For any inquiries, please contact the hospital helpline numbers or email address. Both centers offer Pediatric Cardiology & Cardiac Surgery services. Please note: Foetal Echocardiography services are only available at Atal Nagar.

CONTACT US

FOR ENQUIRIES

To Consult our Doctor kindly <u>Click here</u>
> For general enquiries, contact: <u>info@srisathyasaisanjeevani.com</u>
> For Career enquiries, contact: <u>hr@srisathyasaisanjeevani.com</u>
> For Media enquiries, contact: <u>media@srisathyasaisanjeevani.com</u>
> For Volunteering enquiries, contact: <u>getinvolved@srisathyasaisanjeevani.com</u>

ATAL NAGAR, CHHATTISGARH

Address: Address: Sri Sathya Sai Sanjeevani Center for Child Heart Care Sector 2, Atal Nagar (Naya Raipur) Chhattisgarh – 492101

Contact no. Contact No. (Available Monday – Saturday 9 AM to 5 PM):+918010119000

Email:<u>info.raipur@srisathyasaisanjeevani.com</u>

The Hospital is situated at Atal Nagar (Naya Raipur), at a distance of around 26 km from Raipur Railway Station and 11 km from the Airport. The nearest landmark is International Cricket Stadium and 'Sendh' Lake, at Atal Nagar (Naya Raipur).

Directions to Atal Nagar Hospital

PALWAL, HARYANA

Address: Address: Sri Sathya Sai Sanjeevani International Centre for Child Heart Care & Research Baghola, NH-2, Delhi-Mathura Road, Palwal (District), Haryana – 121102

Contact no. Contact No. (Available Monday – Saturday 9 AM to 5 PM):+918010119000

Email:info.palwal@srisathyasaisanjeevani.com

The Hospital is located on Delhi Mathura Highway on NH2 in the Palwal district of Haryana. The nearest city to the Hospital is Faridabad and the nearest Airport is Indira Gandhi International Airport in New Delhi.

Sri Sathya Sai Institute of Higher Medical Sciences (Totally Free)

Sri Sathya Sai Institute of Higher Medical Sciences, Prasanthigram
PHONE: 08047104600
STATE-OF-THE-ART MEDICAL SERVICE COMPLETELY FREE OF CHARGE

<u>SPECIALITIES</u>
Cardiology, CTVS, Ophthalmology, Plastic Surgery, Gastroenterology, Urology, Orthopaedics

<u>SERVICES</u>
Radiology, Anaesthesiology, Nursing, Laboratory Services, Dietary Services, Blood Bank

<u>CONTACT</u>
Treatment Related - 08555-287388 Extn 1824, enquirypg@sssihms.org.in

General Queries - 08555-287388 Extn 1709, publicrelationspg@sssihms.org.in

Academics Related - 08555-287388 EXTN 1710, academicspg@sssihms.org.in

HOSPITAL HELPLINE NUMBER: 080 47104600
RE-VISIT PATIENTS CAN CONTACT THE SPECIFIC DEPARTMENTS DIRECTLY:
CARDIOLOGY: 08555 281990; UROLOGY: 08555 281992; OPHTHALMOLOGY: 08555 281758;
PLASTIC SURGERY: 08555 281776; ORTHOPAEDICS: 08555 281300.

Patients and attendants, please note: No third-party websites like justdial.com or any other website are allowed to give appointments to patients on its behalf. These appointments are invalid. To taking an appointment please contact the hospital directly.

Important Instructions

All services provided to patients of SSSIHMS, Prasanthigram are totally free of charge. The hospital does not have a billing counter. The hospital strictly confirms a first come first serve policy with provisions for emergency medical conditions. Patients and patient attendants are advised not to pay anyone who claims to be a staff member of SSSIHMS, Prasanthigram for any service whatsoever. Immediately bring details of such individuals to the notice of the Hospital Security. Patients who have visited the hospital once, are given an appointment for a later date by the departments, or visit the hospital on specific instructions of the doctors are known as re-visit patients.

Information for First Visit Patients

It is advisable that patients visit the hospital after taking a prior appointment.

Entering through the Patient Gate

The patient gate lies on the East end of the hospital campus. After entering through the patient's gate, you enter the campus of SSSIHMS, Prasanthigram. Soon after your entry, Sevadal, in blue scarfs, would give you a token for the respective department you have come to visit for treatment. The token number denotes your position in the queue.

You may then proceed to the Screening and Registration Block. Only one attendant will be allowed to enter the campus with a patient.

<u>Screening and Registration Block</u>

At the Screening and Registration Block (SRB), the patients will be directed to the appropriate queues, for Cardiology/CTVS, Urology, Ophthalmology, Orthopaedics, and Plastic Surgery. Gastroenterology patients if any should first visit only the Sri Sathya Sai General Hospital, Puttaparthi and on their referral to the Gastroenterology department in SSSIHMS, they could go to Room No. 124.

In the SRB doctors concerned will evaluate your condition and advise you accordingly. Once advised by the doctors in the SRB to approach the OPD, you will be registered and given a registration card with a specific number after which you may then proceed to the respective OPD in the main hospital.

Also if a person, who has visited a specific department of the hospital earlier, wants to visit another department, then he will be treated as a new patient for the new department. In such a case, the patient has to produce his old registration card when he is being registered for the new department.

Patients are required to bring along a first-degree relative (related by blood) as an attendant to the hospital for the fulfillment of procedural requirements.

When one gets discharged from the hospital they are given instructions to visit the hospital once again after a specified period for a check-up. The revisit date is mentioned at the bottom of the discharge summary. If you fall in this category, then please check your discharge summary to find out when you should visit the hospital again. If any complications arise before your due date for a revisit, please call the respective department and follow the instructions given.

If you have any queries then you can call up the following numbers: Patient correspondence Cell – 08555-287388 Ext-1824. Please dial the phone number given above and also the extension number shown above or you can wait for operator assistance.

For patients who are called for undergoing surgery or a procedure, a letter is sent from the hospital with detailed instructions. Please go through the letter carefully and arrive at the hospital at least one day before the date of appointment.

If a patient is coming for surgery, it is important that he/she gets his/her blood group tested in their hometown.

Appointment

The patients can contact SSSIHMS through e-mail or ordinary post to take an appointment. The covering letter must have the Name, address, and phone number of the patient (Important), Age, and ailment. How long he/she has been suffering from the same. The preferred time during the year, when the patient wants to visit the hospital. (Please note, this is just to know a time convenient for you. The final decision, however, will be made by the specific department only.) Photocopies of previous medical records (if any) are attached to the covering letter (Important).

INSTRUCTIONS:

Please DO NOT send a request (e-mail or post)for an appointment for the same ailment to more than one hospital of Sri Sathya Sai Central Trust. This will result in unnecessary confusion during the processing of your request and delay the reply from our side. Please DO NOT send the appointment request both by e-mail and post. Patients seeking appointments through e-mail are requested to send their request to SSSIHMS, Prasanthigram's patient-related e-mail only – enquirypg@sssihms.org.in. Sending the request to more than one e-mail id will make processing of your request difficult and delay our response. Appointments for two different departments cannot be given on the same day. If a patient seeks an appointment for more than one department, then he/she must send separate emails for each of the departments.

By calling up the hospital, the patient will have a fair idea of how to go about making an appointment, and how soon he/she might get an appointment. He/She, however, will have to send the covering letter and the photocopies of the medical records (if any), through e-mail or post.

Taking appointments through e-mail

For taking appointments through email, the patients have to mail a covering letter along with scanned medical records to the following email id.

enquirypg@sssihms.org.in

Patients sending their covering letter and photocopies of their medical records (if any) will have to send them to:

Patient Correspondence Cell (Room 132), Sri Sathya Sai Institute of Higher Medical Sciences, Prasanthigram, Anantapur District, Andhra Pradesh, PIN: 515134.

Patients who do not have any previous medical records may only send the covering letter with a description of their symptoms.

It is again mentioned that SSSIHMS, Prasanthigram has the specialties of Cardiology, Cardio-Thoracic, Vascular Surgery, Urology, Ophthalmology, Orthopaedics, Plastic Surgery, and Gastroenterology (endoscopy) only. With respect to Gastroenterology (endoscopy), patients should first visit Sri Sathya Sai General Hospital, Puttaparthi, and once referred by the doctors of SSSGH, they should visit the Gastroenterology (endoscopy) department at SSSIHMS.

Once your request for an appointment reaches us, we will get back to you by e-mail or postal address.

All the instructions will be written clearly in the appointment letter mailed to you. Please follow the given instructions.

After your receive the letter, if you have any queries please contact:

Department Phone Number

Patient Correspondence Cell +91-8555-287388 Extension: 1824

Please dial the phone number given above and also the extension number shown above or you can wait for operator assistance. Please call between 8.00 AM and 5.00 PM.

FOR THE ATTENTION OF PATIENTS FROM WEST BENGAL, INDIA

In order to help avoid West Bengal patients from falling prey to touts and to provide better guidance, it is requested that patients wishing to visit the hospital for treatment take an appointment with the hospital and then get a referral letter from the Sri Sathya Sai Seva Organization, West Bengal, before visiting the hospital for treatment. The procedure is as below:

All the patients from West Bengal wishing to avail treatment at SSSIHMS, Prasanthigram, need to make an appointment with the hospital either by post or e-mail (enquirypg@sssihms.org.in) by sending the scanned copies of their medical reports and the scanned copy (or photocopy) of Govt. issued Photo ID card, like the Aadhar Card, Driving License, Voter ID card, etc. or any Govt Id card, which has photo and address of the patient. Receiving an appointment will be a confirmation that the treatment sought by the patient is available at the hospital.

With the appointment letter from the hospital, the patients should visit the respective district president's office of Sri Sathya Sai Seva Organisation for a referral letter. E- mail Id: ssssowb.mail@gmail.com (for information about referral letter and guidance). Interaction with the District President's office helps clarify doubts that the patients may have about the visit to the hospital and also open up a direct line of communication with the Sri Sathya Sai Seva Organisation for the patient so that the patient or attendant can contact the organization any time later also if needed. This helps if some touts try to influence the patient or attendant while they are on their way to the hospital.

The patients should then visit the hospital on the date of appointment with the hospital appointment letter and the referral letter. The patients should carry all their previous medical reports and a valid Govt. Photo Id card.

Patients carrying the appointment and referral letter should directly go to the registration counter for registration skipping the entire screening process. Therefore, they need not stand in the queue for tokens or for screening.

Patients with bone and joint diseases need not get a referral letter from the District president of the Sai Organisation.

Please include the following information while writing for an appointment

a) Name of patient b) Age c) Gender d) Date of Birth e) Current medical problem f) Other diagnosed medical problems

Hospital's Postal address. (Please send us the photocopies only. Do not send Originals.)

Patient Correspondence Cell, Sri Sathya Sai Institute of Higher Medical Sciences, Prasanthigram, Anantapur District, Andhra Pradesh – 515134.

If you are sending the information by post then furnish your complete address, e-mail id if available and mobile number where we can communicate with you if required.

Important instruction for foreign patients

All foreign patients visiting the hospital for treatment must carry a valid Medical Visa.

HOW DO I GET ADMITTED?

Once you are screened, registered, investigated, and diagnosed you may be waitlisted for surgery. You will receive an intimation from the hospital regarding the date for admission. This is not an invitation for admission to the hospital. On the date of admission, you will be completely screened by the doctors. You will be admitted only after you are found fit for surgery or intervention. If found unfit you may not be admitted. Before you start from your residence please follow the checklist given below:

1. Confirm your appointment 2. One attendant is compulsory. The attendant has to be related to the patient by blood. 3. Bring all previous medical records. Both, records from other medical institutions and any medical records given to you by SSSIHMS. 4. To avoid any inconvenience, make your travel arrangements such that you come to the hospital on the appointed day, before 8.30 a.m.

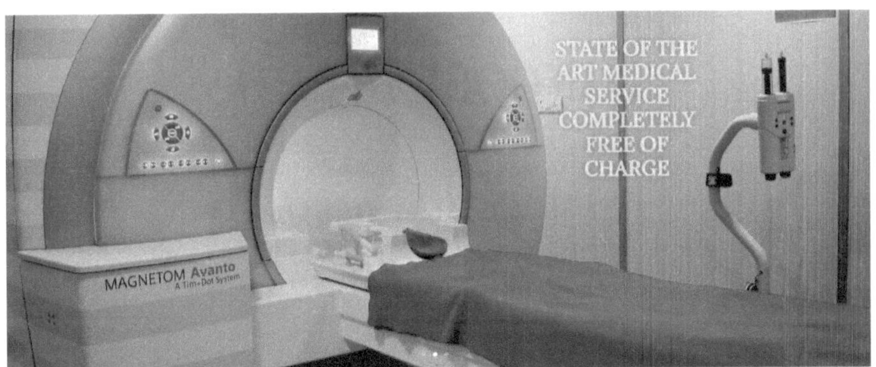

CHAPTER FOUR

TATA MEMORIAL CENTRE
(Almost Free)

TATA MEMORIAL CENTRE (TMC)
Dr. E Borges Road, Parel, Mumbai - 400 012 India
Tel. +91-22- 24177000, 24177300, 24161413
Fax: +91-22-24146937
E-mail :msoffice@tmc.gov.in (for patient care and queries)
feedback@tmc.gov.in (for feedback from patients)
cash@tmc.gov.in (for accounts related)
fundraising@tmc.gov.in (for donors and donation related)
registrar@tmc.gov.in (for education and training)
hrd@tmc.gov.in (for administrative - HRD matters)

Online Form for new patients: https://tmc.gov.in/m_registration/New...

Phone Number to contact Hospital: 022 2417 7000 + Ext.

Tata memorial website: https://tmc.gov.in/

Tata Memorial Hospital was Asia's first cancer research hospital. It is regarded as the best hospital in India. They provide very subsidized treatments.

Full patient guide: https://tmc.gov.in/PDF/Tata_Handbook-...

New Registration Link to Register: https://tmc.gov.in/m_registration/New...

Complete List Of treatment costs: https://tmc.gov.in/tmh/PDF/Schedule_c......

Official Website Of Tata memorial: https://tmc.gov.in/index.php/en/

The Tata Memorial Hospital (TMH) in Mumbai, the Advanced Centre of Treatment Research and Education in Cancer (ACTREC), and the Centre for Cancer Epidemiology (CCE) in Navi Mumbai, form the three distinctive and integral bases of the Tata Memorial Centre (TMC).

TMH is devoted to offering ethical and well-disciplined medical services to cancer patients. ACTREC focuses on basic, translational, and clinical research in cancer. CCE delves into the cause and effect relationship between health, environment, and cancer in our population.

ELEVEN (11) Disease Management Groups (DMGs) that encompass all types of cancers that affect various areas in the human body:

- **Adult Haematolymphoid**
- Bone and Soft Tissue
- Breast
- Gastrointestinal
- Gynecology
- Head and Neck
- Neuro-oncology
- Pediatric Solid Tumors
- Paediatric Haematolymphoid
- Thorax
- Urology

You (general as well as a private patient), who have been newly registered will be seen by a doctor of your DMG on the day of registration itself.

It offers four basic categories to its Out-Patients: General, Private, Outside Referrals (second opinion), and Preventive Oncology. You must be careful when choosing your patient category for treatment in the hospital; a change from one category to another (General to Private or vice versa) is only permitted once.

All investigations will be carried out subject to the rules of the hospital and their schedule of charges. These charges are subject to revision and change from time to time as per hospital policy. Do not pay money to anyone without a valid memo or bill.

Keep in Mind

Outside pathology slides/blocks once submitted will not be returned as routine practice.

For any type of biopsy performed in our hospital, please inform the concerned doctor beforehand if you need to take slides/blocks for an outside opinion; else, they may not be issued to you unless the same procedure is repeated and paid for.

Hard copies of radiological and other imaging investigations done at TMH are available at the cost decided by the management from time to time. The same, on CDs, are given free when required by you, within a month of completion of your investigation. (We do not send any images or reports via email; nor is it our policy to access our mails to retrieve any outside medical data of our patients).

Outside radiological images will be returned. If need be, they could be scanned for future reference. Radiological investigations (for outside referred cases) that require an intravenous injection of any kind will not be permitted without patient registration; a private patient's case file will need to be made for that.

In case of any doubt with regards to the result of previously performed investigations like diagnostic tests including FNAC / Biopsy etc., the procedure no matter how recent may have to be repeated. The preferred payment method at the hospital is the Smart Card. Cash / Credit / Debit cards can be used ONLY to refill the Smart Card. Cheques are accepted subject to realization. All payments are to be made at the designated cash counters around the hospital (see section 9).

Charges are refunded fully (100%) in cases where the necessary investigation/procedure has not been performed for any reason. They do not take responsibility for any complications that arise from treatment (during or after) taken outside our institution, even if so prescribed by us.

3. Dos and Do not:- NO SMOKING, NO LITTERING, NO CHEWING OR SPITTING OF TOBACCO / PAAN MASALA / GUTHKA, NO ALCOHOL CONSUMPTION, NO COCONUT SHELL ON PREMISES, MAINTAIN HYGIENE.

Keep hands clean at all times, especially when visiting those who are admitted to the hospital.

Amenities Provided

24-hour ATM: The machines are located on the ground floor and first floor of the Homi Bhabha Building and near the security counter of the Golden Jubilee Building. There is a branch of the Central Bank of India in the basement of the Main Building that is open from 0930 – 1415 hours (Monday – Friday) and from 0930 - 1200 hours (Saturdays) for the benefit of our patients and staff.

Eateries: Canteen within the Annex Building compound: Monday - Friday: 0730 – 1730 hours Saturdays: 0800 – 1415 hours. TAJSATS cafeteria at the Homi Bhabha Building, 1st floor: Monday - Friday: 0900 – 1730 hours Saturdays: 0900 – 1300 hours.

Electronic Kiosks: For self-registration and Electronic Medical Report information, kiosks are located between Annex & Golden Jubilee Building;

1st, 2nd & 3rd floor of Homi Bhabha Building; 3rd floor of Service Building and ground floor of Main Building.

Elevators: Each building has elevators for the convenience of staff and patients. Do not use the smaller elevators; they are meant exclusively for our staff. All are advised to use these amenities keeping in mind the need and urgency of the patients and staff first.

Helpline and Helpdesk: Golden Jubilee basement and Homi Bhabha Building 1st floor (Rotunda). Information Booklets about cancer are available in the compound of the Annex Building and at the Homi Bhabha Building, 1st floor (Rotunda). Mobile Services: MTNL network works best on the campus; other services depend on areas within the campus.

Printing Facilities: Any report (diagnostic, therapeutic, or treatment-related) for all patients in our institution may be printed on the 1st floor of the Golden Jubilee Building and Homi Bhabha Building at the cost of ` 3 per report. A storage facility is available for luggage. A cloakroom is present behind the Golden Jubilee Building, on the ground floor where any registered patient can leave their luggage. The storage is open and there is a security guard present to ensure the safety of your luggage.

Toilets: There are separate toilets for men and women on each floor. For directions, please ask any staff member. In each building, most of the locations of the toilets are the same on every floor. Handicap Toilets: They are situated in the Golden Jubilee basement, to the left of room number 9, and in the Homi Bhabha Building, first floor, near the TAJSATS cafeteria.

<u>Bring Along</u>

Companion: You should have a responsible adult attendant who will assist you, and can make decisions on your behalf if you are unable to do so.

Documents: For Indian citizens, a referral letter from your referring doctor/institution is mandatory.

For foreign nationals: An original passport with a valid medical visa is mandatory. (All foreign patients must be accompanied by a person carrying an original passport and a valid medical attendant visa).

Documents related to medical insurance, any charitable funding, and health claims should be photocopied and attested by the Public Relations Office (Homi Bhabha Building, 1st floor, counter 123).

Food: Please carry something light and dry to eat, as it may be a long wait for your appointment on crowded days at the hospital.

Passing time: During your wait, keep yourself occupied with some reading material; please carry small portable games for children to pass their time.

Reports: Please carry reports of radiology, imaging, blood tests, pathology slides, or blocks. Hard or soft copies of the same, if available, would help. (Please photocopy all documents and future transactions performed in our institution for your record).

Various Patient Categories

Depending on your financial capacity to pay for treatment at Tata Memorial Hospital, you will fall under one of the following categories:

General Patients (Part paying):

All patients fall under the 'C category' till their subsequent category is determined by the medical social worker or the office of the Medical Superintendent.

Categories:

C: Partly charged (20% for investigations and consultations and the rest as per actuals).

NC: Minimal charges for a few services; no investigation or consultation charges and the rest as per actuals.

BP (Below poverty): The Rajeev Gandhi Jeevan Yojana Scheme (RGJYS) provides cashless quality care to families with an annual income below ` 1,00,000 for an amount of ` 1,50,000 per family per year.

Private Patients (Full paying):

Categories:

B: Indian citizen

F: Foreign national

Do remember that all services for all patient categories are provided at subsidized rates.

Registration Hours (general-GJB-G-55 or private- HBB-125_127): Monday - Friday: 0800 - 1400 hours Saturday: 0800 - 1215 hours . Cash Counter (GJB-111 and at HBB-136,137): Monday - Friday: 0800 - 1900 hours Saturdays: 0800 - 1400 hours . After office hours, cash payment may be made at MB-G-77.

Blood & Sample Collection / Deposition: General Patients: Monday - Friday GJB-123: 0700 - 1430 hours

Saturday HBB-101,102: 0700 - 1230 hours . Private and RF Category: HBB-101, 102: Monday - Friday: 0700 - 1430 hours. Saturday: 0700 - 1130 hours. After office hours, the above services are provided at MB-G-77.

Radiodiagnosis (general-GJB-B-3 or private-MB-G-64): Monday – Friday: 0930 - 1900 hours Saturdays: 0930 - 1400 hours

Dispensary:

MB-B-28: 24 hours

MB-202: 0700 – 2100 hours

HBB-G-51: 0700 – 1900 hours

Administrative Hours:

Monday - Friday: 0930 - 1730 hours Saturday: 0930 - 1415 hours

Emergency:

Casualty services are available at MB-G-77 round the clock. All emergency payments and, blood or sample deposits (for all categories of patients) are to be made hereafter official hours.

Blood Donation SB-602:

Eligible adults are encouraged to donate blood. Kindly contact the MSW (GJB-G-54) or any blood bank staff prior to blood donation.

Services after official hours:

Blood Collection MB-G-77

Radiological Services MB-G-66

Free Shuttle Service:

Between TMH (Parel) and ACTREC (Kharghar)

From TMH: 0830, 1030, 1100, 1430 and 1800 hours.

From ACTREC: 0830, 1300, 1400, 1600, and 1800 hours.

<u>Registration (for all categories)</u> :

This process could take up to one hour. If you are a holder of the earlier cardboard card, a new plastic Smart Card bearing the same case file number will have to be made at the registration counter (GJB-G-55 for general patients; HBB-125_127 for private patients). You may be required to deposit money in your new Smart Card.

Old case files may be collected from GJB-G-55 or the DMG secretary. Please come to the hospital for registration with your referral letter and with reports of previous investigations (if any).

The REGISTRATION process for General patients (GJB-G-55) and Private Patients (HBB-125_127) can be expedited as the hospital provides the facility to register online from any location, as well as on-site from the electronic kiosks (refer to page 41 for location). All categories of patients can avail themselves of this registration facility. Kindly go to https://tmc.gov.in and click on 'Online patient services' to begin the registration process. A provisional registration number will be issued to you. The acknowledgment that comes from our institution after successful completion of online registration also provides you with a password. This password is private and is meant for you to change any mistake made in the registration details that were entered earlier. With this provisional number, proceed to the registration counter directly (GJB-G-55 or HBB-125_127).

If you have not registered online, go to the GJB-G-50 (general patients) or HBB-125_127 (private patients – Indian and foreign nationals) to fill out a form, take the token number, and proceed to the registration counter when called for.

Ensure that your nearest airport /railway station/bus depot is entered correctly in the registration form to avail of travel concession.

Hospitalization

If your doctor has advised hospitalization for further medical management, visit the admission counter (HBB-131_133). The process of hospitalization (admission) can take up to 2 weeks. In cases where surgery is contemplated, the date given by the surgeon may not match that given by the admission office for the room; be prepared to be admitted to the hospital for a week prior to the actual date of surgery. As soon as a bed is available, you will be informed depending on your wait-list number. Check for the same after 1500 hours on any day for confirmation, if the admission office has not contacted you.

You have a choice of rooms while staying in the hospital. General Patients of different genders are admitted in separate wards in MB. Private Patients have a choice of:

B: Semi-Private Room (2 / 3 patients in a room)

A: Private Room (Single occupancy)

D: Deluxe Room (Single occupancy)

Hospital Deposit: You have to pay a deposit at the time of admission depending on the choice of room. This deposit is adjusted with the final bill; the balance, if any, will be refunded. Any excess in billing will have to be paid.

GENERAL PATIENTS:

C Category: Hospital Deposit - ` 5000

NC Category: No fee

PRIVATE PATIENTS:

Semi private (B category):

Hospital Deposit: ` 35,000; Bed cost: ` 1,900/ day.

Private (A category):

Hospital Deposit: ` 50,000; Bed cost: ` 3,500/ day.

Private Deluxe (D category):

Hospital Deposit: ` 75,000; Bed cost: ` 4,800/ day

Foreign patient (F):

Hospital Deposit: ` 2,00,000; Bed cost: ` 4800/ day

Medical procedures are costlier in the private category.

One pass for an attendant is always given to you for any category that is valid throughout your stay in the hospital.

Discharge Procedure:

The consulting doctor will advise you / your family of when you are permitted to leave the hospital. This information is generally disclosed 24 hours before discharge. You are requested to leave the hospital by 1300 hours on the day of discharge so that we can arrange for the admission of another patient.

Discharge card: One of our senior doctors will prepare a discharge card containing a summary of all the investigations and treatments performed on you in our hospital, as well as advice on discharge and follow-up. Please go through the discharge card carefully and clear all queries and concerns with your DMG doctors. If you are planning to stay at St. Judes, Borges Memorial Home, or any other affiliated institution, you are required to present your discharge card at the time of admission.

Other Useful Departments:

Day Care: The day-care center is open to you (general or private) if you require intravenous fluids, chemotherapy, blood product, or transfusion (0700 – 2100 hours). General patients: MB-523 , Private patients: HBB-501_514 , Paediatric patients: MB-524 and AB-1100

Dental Department: Dental Care is provided if you are suffering from any dental-related issues. You are offered prophylactic treatment along with dental prosthesis, post-surgery. General patients: GJB-121, Private patients: HBB-217

General Medicine (Physician): The facilities include- Echocardiography and stress tests (MB-105).Pulmonary function test (HBB-G-69).

Nutritional Clinic: This department provides dietary advice as per the needs of the patient. General patients: GJB-101, Private patients: HBB-319

Occupational and Physiotherapy: They help you to recover from prolonged immobilization and also suggest various exercises to preserve your body function. All patients: MB-G-94,96

Pain Clinic: This department caters to patients suffering from intractable pain. General patients: GJB-B-19, Private patients: HBB-G-71

Palliative Care: All patients: MB-B-75

Psychiatry and Psychology: This department provides emotional support to you and your family through any stage of your disease.

Referrals from doctors or any other professional as well as self-referrals are also looked into. General patients: GJB-B-18, Private patients: HBB-G-68

Pulmonary Medical Unit (Chest Physician): This department is located at GJB-B-13, for respiratory problems of any patient during official working hours from Monday - Friday only.

Speech Therapy: Helps to re-develop your speech after surgery GJB-B-9.

Transfusion Medicine SB-501: Blood shall be provided to you, where it is indicated. The blood shall be screened for HIV, Hepatitis B and C, syphilis, and malaria. Only compatible blood is issued to you. Blood for surgery is available to patients at all times.

<u>Accommodation</u>

If you are an adult, the Medical Social Workers' Department also arranges for free or subsidized accommodation at the Borges Memorial Home in Bandra and other sites. Accommodation is provided for both general and private categories of patients on a first-come-first-serve basis. You have to present your Tata Memorial Hospital Smart Card and discharge card to be allowed admission. The length of stay permitted is 4 to 6 weeks and is applicable only for those on close regular follow-up.

The St Jude India ChildCare Centres provides accommodation & support to children and their parents through its well-established model of cost-free, holistic care during the period of the child's treatment. Here too, one has to present their Tata Memorial Hospital Smart Card and discharge card to be allowed admission.

You could receive financial aid from philanthropic institutions; the account of the same will be maintained by the Medical Social Worker's department. The cost of your treatment will be deducted from this account as and when incurred. For any subsidization or concession, the final authority lies in the hands of the Medical Social Workers' department. All documents will have to be submitted to them and all approvals need to be taken from them.

<u>How to reach</u>

Please keep in mind that there will be traffic while coming to TMH. Plan your journey in advance, in order to be on time for your appointment.

Wheelchairs and stretchers are available at the entrances of the Main Building, the Homi Bhabha Building, and the Golden Jubilee Building.

Telephone numbers of ambulance services (depending on the destination and/or origin) are provided by our telephone operator on the Main Building ground floor (dial #9 from our intercom or +91 22 24177000 from outside). The cost of the services has to be decided by you with the service provider.

Address: Tata Memorial Hospital, Dr. E. Borges Road, Parel (East), Mumbai - 400 012, India

Telephone: +91 22 2417 7000 / 7300

Fax: +91 22 24146937

Email: msoffice@tmc.gov.in

Website: https://tmc.gov.in

Bus Stops:

Bhoiwada: 9, 14, 61, 64, 67, 73, 166, 168, 200, 216.

Haffkine: 40Ltd, 57, 69, 73, 134, 160, 162, 201,212, 213, 216, 368Ltd.

KEM Hospital: 9, 14, 57, 61, 64, 67, 69, 134, 166.

Parel: 1, 4Ltd, 5, 6Ltd, 7Ltd, 15, 19Ltd, 21Ltd, 22Ltd, 25Ltd, 30Ltd, 40Ltd, 43, 51, 54, 66, 76, 160, 162, 163, 168, 201, 212, 213, 368Ltd, 506Ltd, 961a/c.

Wadia Hospital: 9, 14, 40 Ltd, 57, 64, 67, 134, 160, 162, 200, 212, 213, 216, 368 Ltd.

Kindly check the latest bus routes from local authorities

Trains:

Western Railway (WR) - Elphinstone

Central Railway (CR) - Parel; Harbour Line - Sewri

Monorail:

From Chembur, Wadala, and Jacob Circle (Mahalaxmi) to TMH.

Chhatrapati Shivaji International Airport:

Terminal 1 - Domestic, Santacruz

Terminal 2 - International, Andheri

Other transports like shared taxi services between Dadar TT (train station) and our hospital are available.

There is a free shuttle service between Dadar TT (train station) to TMH (outside Annex Building) daily from 0800 - 1830 hours.

There are many hotels, restaurants, lodging, and boarding places in the vicinity of our campus that could be of use to you. Some charitable trusts also supply breakfast daily to our patients on the footpath of our Main Building facing the Annex Building.

Numerous chemist stores in our vicinity could be useful in case any medication is out of stock, within the hospital dispensaries.

Children, General, Maternity, and Orthopaedic hospitals are also within walking distance from our hospital.

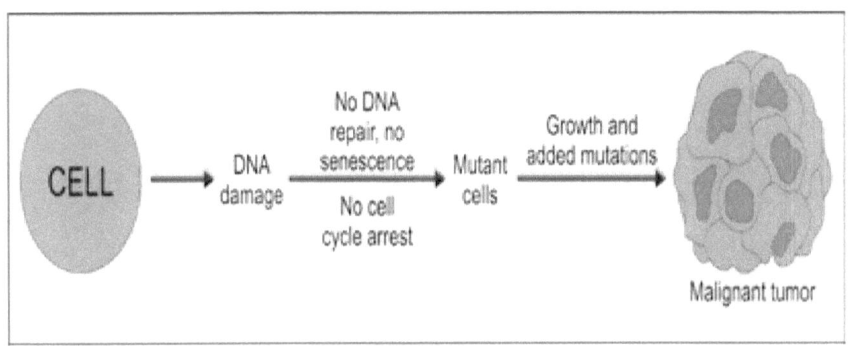

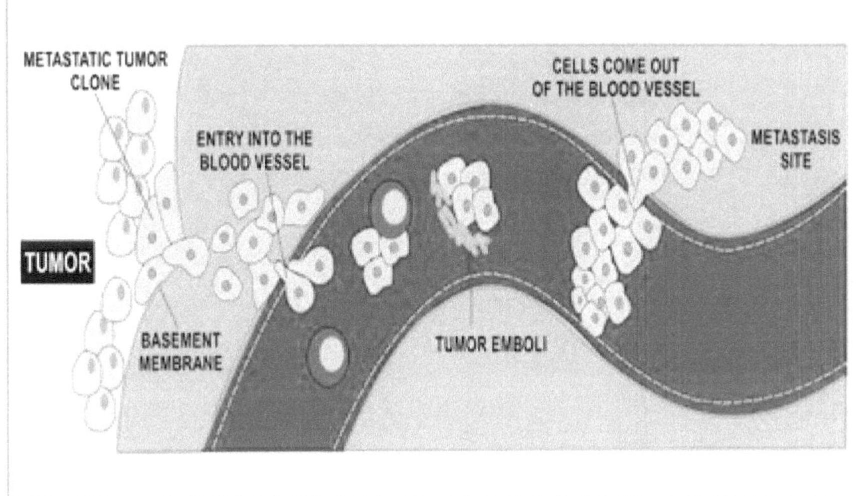

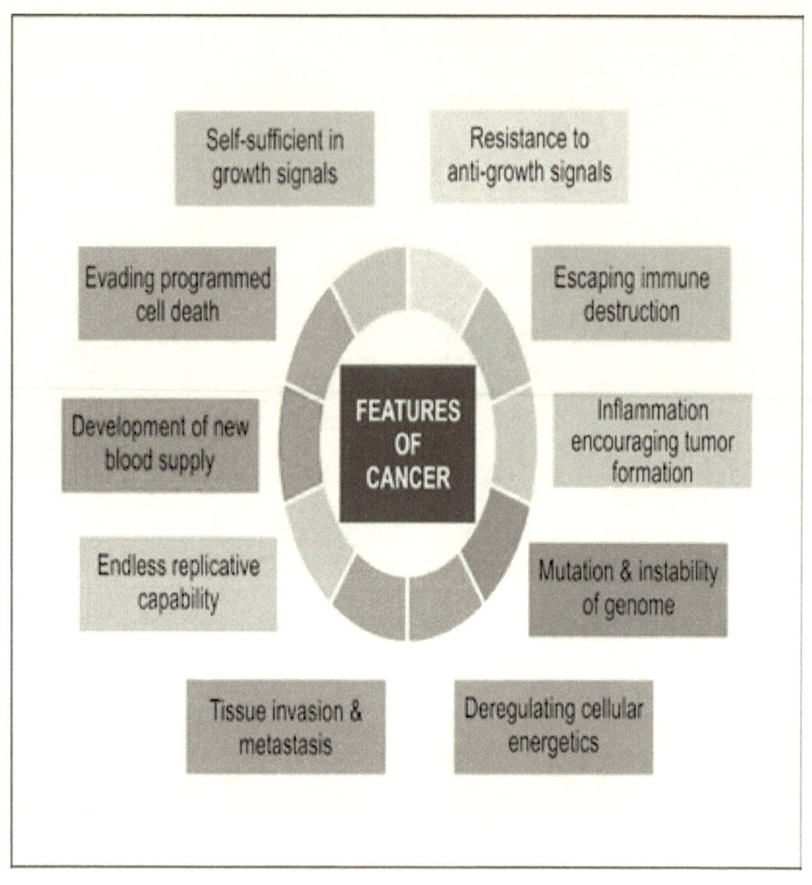
Self-sufficient in
growth signals
Resistance to
anti-growth signals
Evading programmed
cell death
Escaping immune
destruction
FEATURES
OF
CANCER
Development of new
blood supply
Inflammation
encouraging tumor
formation
Endless replicative
capability
Mutation & instability
of genome
Tissue invasion &
metastasis
Deregulating cellular
energetics

Kidney Dialysis Hospital(Totally Free)

The Guru Harkrishan Institute of Medical Sciences and Research's (With 100 beds, no billing counter, free dialysis center at Delhi Gurdwara)

The biggest problem faced by kidney patients is dialysis. There are not many hospitals for dialysis and a significant amount is charged in private hospitals. In such a situation, in order to provide great relief to the patients, the Delhi Sikh Gurdwara Management Committee (DSGMC) has opened the country's largest kidney dialysis hospital at Gurdwara Bala Sahib. This hospital was inaugurated by Gurdwara Committee officials and Ragi-jathas in the presence of Sri Guru Granth Sahib. Let us know what the arrangement for the patients in this hospital is.

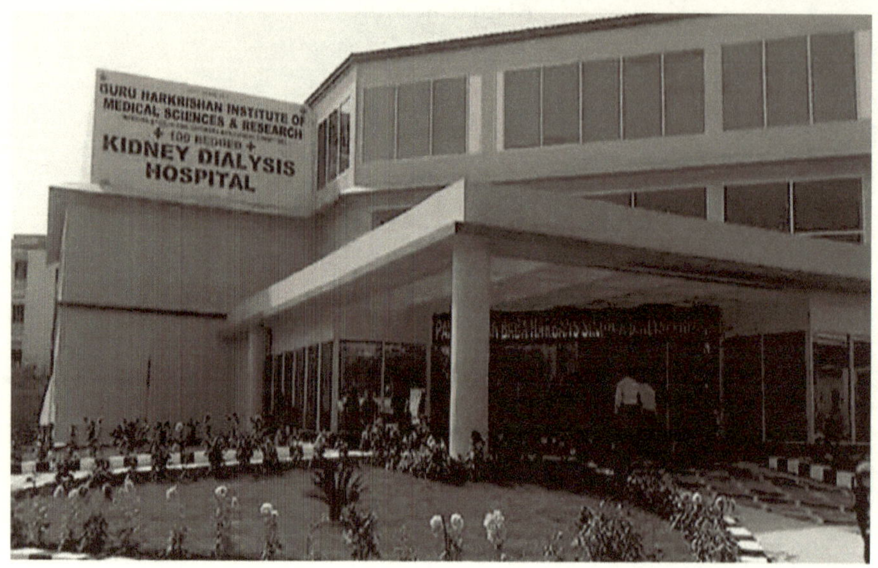

Where is this hospital? How long will you get the treatment?

Guru Harkishan Hospital is coming up in the historic Gurdwara Bala Sahib. A 100-bedded dialysis block has been started in the first phase. This block has been named after Baba Harbans Singhji of Kar Seva. This hospital will be 24x7.

What are the facilities in the hospital?

There is a round-the-clock arrangement of kidney dialysis. Along with this, the hospital will also make arrangements for the food of the patients. In the dialysis block, private rooms have been made keeping in mind the corona patient from the private ward. From the block to these rooms, LED units have been installed on which live telecast of Delhi and other historical Gurdwaras of the country will be done.

What is the capacity of this kidney dialysis hospital?

DSGMC President Manjinder Singh Sirsa said that 100 people can get dialysis done at a time in this hospital. Here are 50 of the electric chairs found in airplane business class. This has been done so that during dialysis, if a patient feels boredom or discomfort in the bed, then he can also sit on the chair.

What technology will be used in this hospital?

According to Sirsa, the kidney dialysis hospital is equipped with hi-tech facilities. The machines and all the equipment installed here are imported from Germany. All the machines are modern as well as equipped with the latest technology.

How much will the fee for registration be? How much will the treatment cost?

The most important thing about the hospital is that it is equipped with modern facilities and is completely free for the patients. The Gurdwara Committee claims that this is the first hospital in the world that will not have a 'cash counter'. Patients will only have to register and the treatment will be free of cost as well as their food will also be arranged 24x7 in the hospital.

Speaking to NDTV, Manjinder Singh Sirsa, DSGMC chief, said, "The purpose of this hospital is to serve humanity. The Sikh community is known for this. Soon, we will be placing 1000 beds in the next year."

With a team of 90 Para medics and 24 doctors working round the clock, the hospital hopes to serve all with minimum formalities, emphasized Dr. Venkatesh.

"We can take up in a day 500 patients for dialysis. We will not be asking for any kind of documents or registration from the patients, just like they walk in and out for langars they are welcome to walk in and out for dialysis treatment," he said.

The primary source of funds to run the hospital will be entirely dependent on donations and CSR contributions. "People have donated machines worth ? 10 core. We are receiving funds through donations, not just Sikhs but people of other communities are also coming forward to contribute. We are also receiving funds from the CSR, and government schemes but will not be taking a single penny from patients."

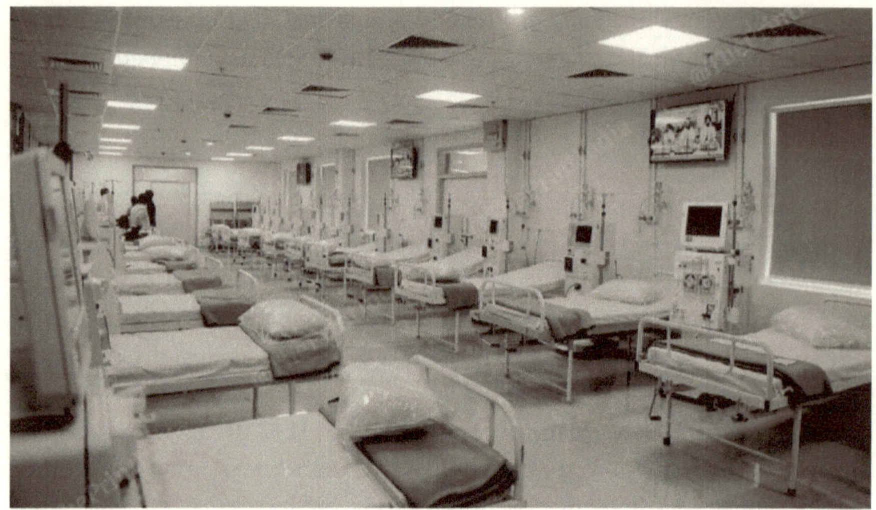

The 100-bed dialysis facility at Guru Harkrishan Institute of Medical Sciences and Research Kidney Dialysis Hospital at Delhi's Gurdwara Bala Sahib

The diagnostic center will open soon. A polyclinic is being started in Gurdwara Bangla Sahib, where the world's cheapest MRI will be available for just Rs 50, and CT scan, X-ray, ultrasound, and dialysis can be done. It will be officially inaugurated on March 11. Thousands of patients arrived for registration. Thousands of patients reached the country's largest kidney dialysis hospital started in Gurdwara Bala Sahib for registration.

Directions to Guru Harkishan Hospital (Delhi) with public transportation

The following transit lines have routes that pass near Guru Harkishan Hospital

- Bus: 306, 323, 396, 473A, 534, 542, 543A, 611, 711, AC-567
- Train: EMU 64012, EMU 64078, EMU 64094
- Metro: PINK LINE

Bus stations near Guru Harkishan Hospital in Delhi

Station Name Distance

Bala Sahib Gurudwara 4 min walk

Gurudwara Bala Sahib 4 min walk

Sarai Kale Khan I.S.B.T 11 min walk

Sarai Kale Khan ISBT 12 min walk

Maharani Bagh / Ashram 13 min walk

Maharani Bagh (Ashram) 13 min a walk
Train stations near Guru Harkishan Hospital in Delhi
Station Name Distance
Lajpat Nagar 4 min walk
Hazrat Nizamuddin 34 min walk
Metro stations near Guru Harkishan Hospital in Delhi
Station Name Distance
Ashram 15 min walk

See Guru Harkishan Hospital, Delhi, on the map

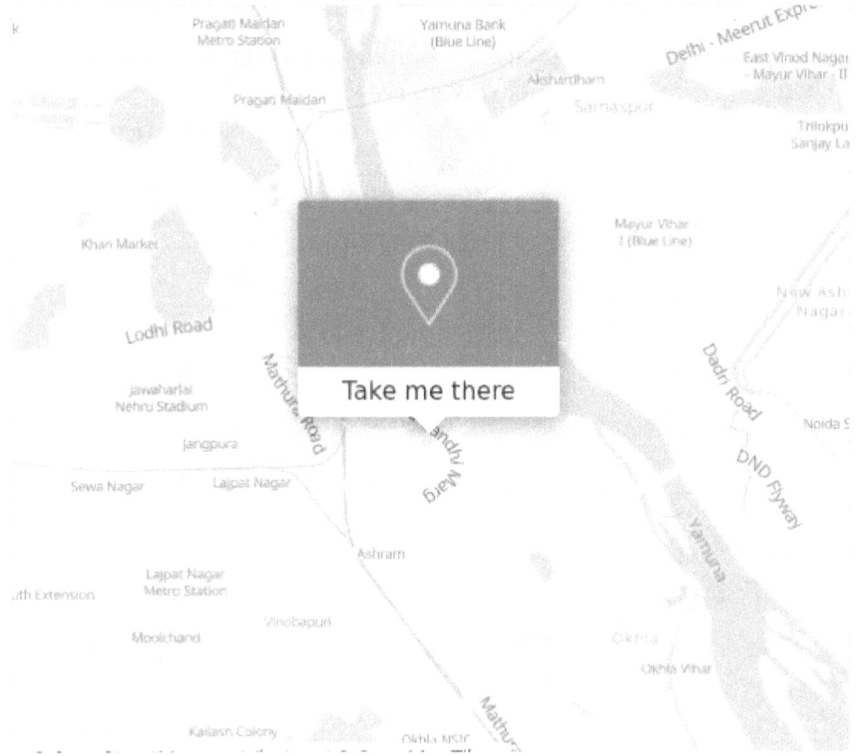

CHAPTER SIX

Guru Ka Langar Eye Hospital(Totally Free)

Guru Ka Langar Eye Hospital (A hospital, where treatment, living, food, and drink all are free.)
Chandigarh Sector 18b, Chandigarh - 160018, Opposite New Public School, Eye Hospitals
PHONE - 1722771171, +919814004184, +919592064040, +917009447390

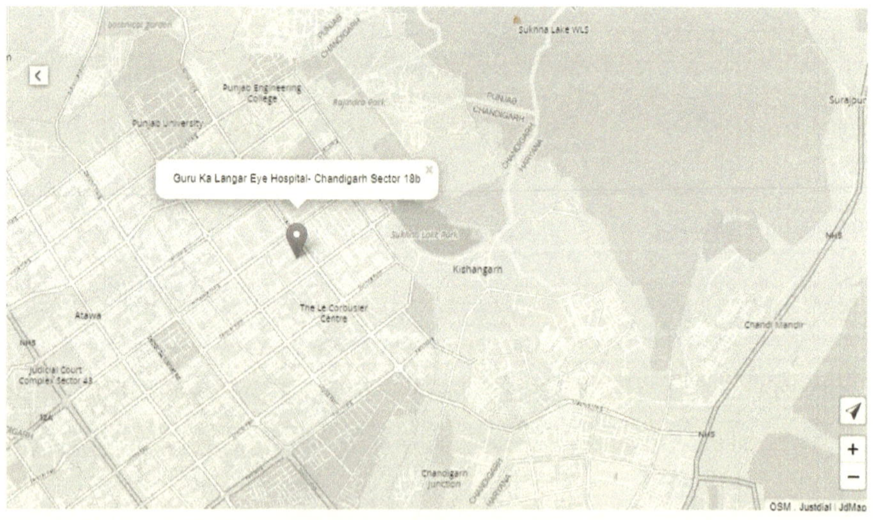

ADDRESS:
Guru Ka Langar Eye Hospital, Opposite New Public School, Sector 18, Chandigarh.

PHONE: 0172-2771171, 9814017102, 9592064040
EMAIL: sewasimran2004@yahoo.co.in
WEBSITE: www.gurukalangareyehospital.in

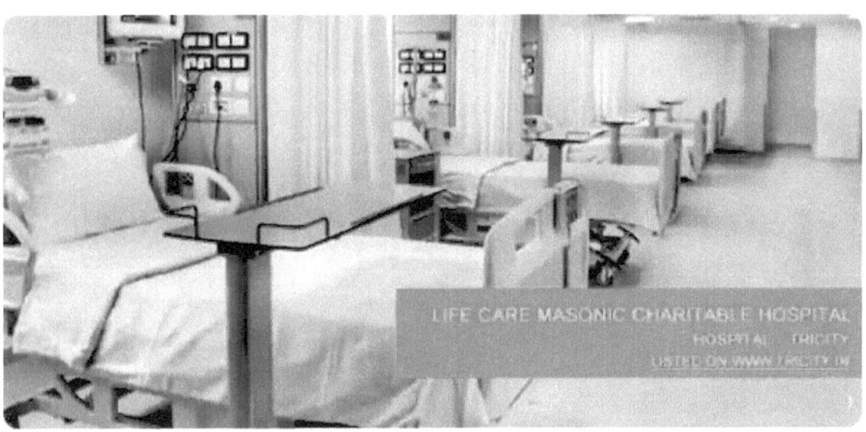

Working Details

Registration Timings: Monday - Saturday: 08:00AM to 10:00AM

Enquiry Timings: Monday - Saturday: 09:00AM to 05:00PM (Closed on Sunday & National Holidays).

Contact Details : 0172 2771171 , +91 95920 64040 , +91 98140 17102

Email: sewasimran2004@yahoo.co.in   ,   Website: www.gurukalangareyehospital.in

1. Which is the nearest landmark?

You can easily locate the establishment as it is in close proximity to Opposite New Public School

2. What are its hours of operation?

The establishment is functional on:

Monday: - Open 24 Hrs

Tuesday: - Open 24 Hrs

Wednesday: - Open 24 Hrs

Thursday:- Open 24 Hrs

Friday: - Open 24 Hrs

Saturday: - Open 24 Hrs

Sunday: - Open 24 Hrs

A hospital, where treatment, living, food, and drink all are free. Not a single penny will have to be spent. If not, click to read full details.

The eye hospital being run under the name Guru Ka Langar in Chandigarh Sector-18 is in the discussion. In this hospital run by Sri Guru Granth Sahib Seva Society, it has been claimed that not only cataracts but retinal operations will be done free of cost. According to the hospital, 25 cataract operations are being done daily at this place for free.

Not only this, arrangements are being made for travel and accommodation for the needy coming from far away. Retina operation also started. Punjab Health Minister Brahm Mohindra inaugurated the retina block. This hospital is located opposite Sector-18 B of the New Public School.

Retina treatment cost 50 thousand, but will be free:

Treatment of retina-related diseases will be done absolutely free in the eye hospital being run from Guru's Langar. The cost of its treatment in any other hospital comes to about 50 thousand rupees. It has been told that USA doctor Harvinder Jeet Singh has donated a machine worth Rs 70 lakh for retina surgery. A retinal microscope machine worth Rs 30 lakh has also arrived. 24 hours free ambulance facility is also available.

Free langar to one thousand people daily:

The officials associated with the trust say that there is an OPD of 500 patients daily in Guru's langar, attendants also accompany them, in such a situation arrangements are made for food and drink for all of them. At one o'clock in the afternoon, langar is arranged for about 800 to one thousand people. After the eye operation, the patients are accommodated in PGI's Infosys-Rotary Sarai. This inn is an air conditioner.

Patients arriving from all over the country:

The message of Guru Ka Langar is spread across the country. Patients from Jammu and Kashmir to Bhopal are reaching Sector-18. A video of Guru Ka Langar is going viral on social media for the past several days. After that people are reaching Chandigarh. Patients will have to register themselves first upon arrival here. After that, the healing process starts. Health Minister Brahm Mohindra while praising this organization for the eyes said that it is a unique experience in his life and he is very happy that this institution is not only treating the eyes of the patients but also providing them with food and drink. They also arrange all for absolutely free.

CHAPTER SEVEN

PILES FREE WORLD HOSPITALS

PILES FREE WORLD HOSPITALS
Hospital in Navi Mumbai, Maharashtra
http://pilesfreeworldhospital.in/
<u>Address</u>: Shop No. 107, Chandrai Arcade, Plot No. A 12, 24,25,26, Near SBI Bank, opposite Railway Station, Sector 20, Nerul West, Navi Mumbai, Maharashtra 400706
<u>Phone</u>: <u>090823 32830</u>

As a result of 40 years of research, the hospital has their formally approved injection which can cure piles, anal Fistula & Rectal prolapse. In the past twenty years, they have curved over a lakh of patients with the use of this treatment.

Moreover, there has been no relapse of this disease. They offer a lifetime cure guarantee which is also unique in the medical world.

Since this injection is based on Ayurveda it has no adverse side reactions.

It obtained a patent (patent no. 216300) in 2008 not only in India but throughout the world. There is no better or more effective cure for piles, Anal fistula & rectal prolapse.

Piles

Piles, also called hemorrhoids are caused as a result of bulging of veins in the lower part of the anus and rectum. When the veins bulge, the walls of the veins get stretched, irritated, and bleed. Piles are classified into internal and external types. As the name suggests, internal piles occur inside the anal canal. They can grow and come out of the anus sometimes. External piles grow at the very end of the anus.

Fistula

There are different treatment options for anal fistula, depending on the severity. Today, fistula is, First time in India unique technique for the treatment of Fistula without surgery, without laser, and without Ksharsutra. They can treat fistula with our government of India's Patented injection/applicators. There is no need to stay in hospital. Only 20 min procedure and no recurrence of fistula in whole life.

First Time In India Latest Advanced Piles Treatment, Without Surgery / Without Ksharsutra / Without Laser Only 20 Min. Procedure.

No Admission, No, Stay In Hospital

PUNE BRANCH

Address: Plot No. 177, Saykar Building, Opposite Sai Multispeciality Hospital, Near Sane Chowk, Akurdi-Chikhali Road, Chinchwad, Pune - 411019.

Phone : +91 9112675901 / 7038569384

MUMBAI BRANCH

Address: Shop No. 107, Chandrai Arcade, Plot No. A 12, 24,25,26, Near SBI Bank, Opposite Railway Station, Sector 20, Nerul West, Navi Mumbai, 400706.

Phone : +91 9112675901 / +91 9082332830

Need An Emergecny Help <u>+91 9112675901</u>

As a result of 40 years of research, they have with their formally approved injection can cure piles, anal Fistula & Rectal prolapse.

<u>Service</u>

- <u>Piles Treatment In Pune</u>
- <u>Fistula Treatment In Pune</u>
- <u>Piles Treatment In Navi Mumbai</u>
- <u>Fistula Treatment In Navi Mumbai</u>

<u>Get In Touch</u>

- +91 9112675901 / 7038569384
- Info@Pilesfreeworld.Com
- Plot No. 177, Saykar Building, Opposite Sai Multispeciality Hospital, Near Sane Chowk, Akurdi-Chikhali Road, Chinchwad, Pune - 411019.

PUNE BRANCH

Address : Plot No. 177, Saykar Building, Opposit Sai Multispeciality Hospital, Near Sane Chowk, Akurdi-Chikhali Road, Chinchwad, Pune - 411019.

Phone   +91 9112675901 / 7038569384

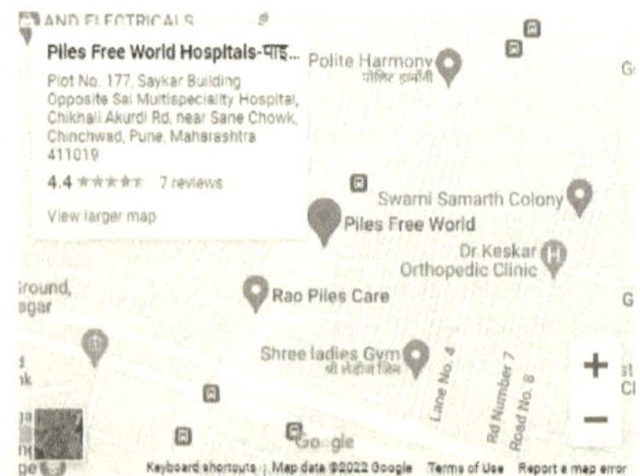

MUMBAI BRANCH

Address : Shop No. 107, Chandrai Arcade, Plot No. A 12, 24,25,26, Near SBI Bank, Opposite Railway Station, Sector 20, Nerul West, Navi Mumbai, 400706.

Phone : +91 9112675901 / +91 9082332830

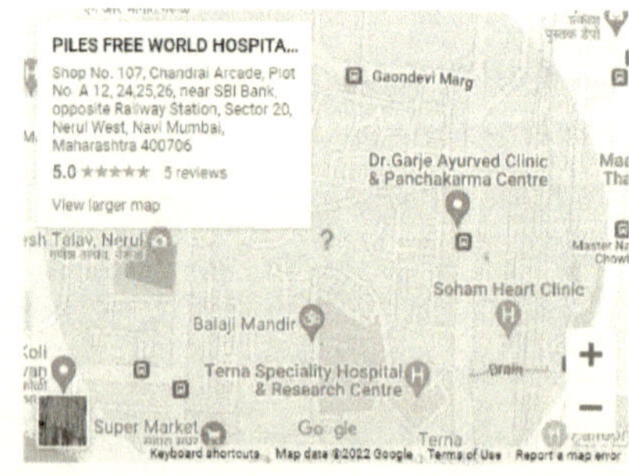

Piles

Piles, also called haemorrhoids are caused as a result of bulging of veins in the lower part of the anus and rectum. When the veins bulge, the walls of the veins gets stretched, irritated and bleed. Piles are classified into internal and external types. As the name suggests, internal piles occur inside the anal canal. They can grow and come out of the anus some times. External piles grow at the very end of the anus.

Call Now For Pune Branch >

Call Now For Navi Mumbai Branch >

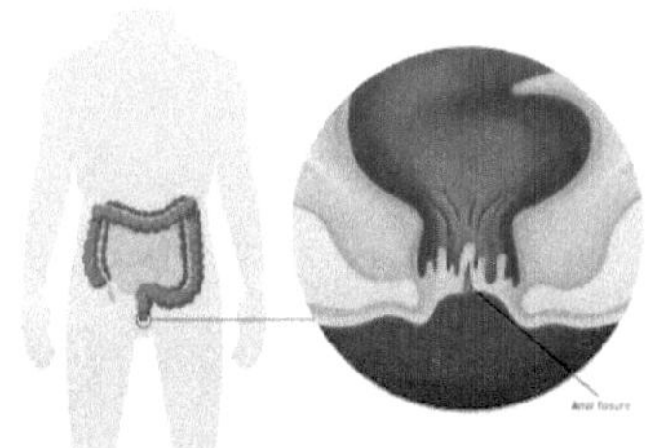

Fistula

There are different treatment options for anal fistula, depending on the severity. Today, for fistula. First time in india unique technique for treatment of Fistula without surgery, without laser, without Ksharsutra, we can treat fistula with our government of india Patented injuction / aplicators. their is no need to stay in hospital. only 20 min procedure and no recurrence of fistula in whole life

Call Now For Pune Branch >

Call Now For Navi Mumbai Branch >

CHAPTER EIGHT

Christian Medical College and Hospital (CMC Vellore)

<u>Christian Medical College and Hospital (CMC Vellore)</u>
Address: Christian Medical College, IDA Scudder Rd, Sripuram,
Beripettai, Vellore, Tamil Nadu 632004; Phone: 094987 60000.

Christian Medical College and Hospital (CMC Vellore) is an educational and research institution and a third-care hospital located in Tamil Nadu, India. It is one of the prominent and well-known medical destinations in India of national and international repute. It is also one of the top-ranked medical colleges in India.

This is a 116-year-old CMC hospital. The founder of the hospital is Ida Sophia Scudder. The idea of starting this hospital established in 1900 is even earlier. In 1890, Ida Sophia Scudder traveled from the United States to South India to visit her missionary parents. One night, three pregnant women from different areas were asked to help give birth. Ida had no training. She wants her father's help. Dad was also a doctor. But none of the families of the three women agreed to seek medical treatment from a male doctor. The next morning the three women died.

Ida was severely and emotionally traumatized. She could not accept the death of three women due to social barriers. She swore to be a doctor. She vowed to serve women and children. Ida then returned to the United States. She graduated from Cornell University Medical College in 1899. That was the first batch of female students there. Witnessing the death of women due to the lack of a female doctor convinced Ida Sophia that God wanted her to become a **female physician** to help the women of India. She never married and stayed single throughout her life to fulfill her mission. Ida returned to India in 1900. She started the hospital with a single bed in her father's house. Now there are more than two thousand inpatients in CMC and seven thousand outpatients daily.

Many patients go to Vellore for every year treatment from the state of West Bengal. But with so many hospitals in the state, why do they crowd the Deccan? Retired Justice Asim Bandyopadhyay, chairman of the state health commission, told in a hearing that "the answer to so many crowds is hidden in Vellore, on the hospital bill." Therefore, a sample of the medical bill of a patient in the state will be sent to all the private hospitals in the state to be cured by treatment at the Christian Medical College. The decision of the Health Commission is based on the complaint made by Bikash Chandra Mandal, a resident of North 24 Parganas.

Bikash told the Health Commission that he was injured in a bike accident in Barrackpore. Get first aid and examination at two local hospitals. He was later admitted to a private hospital on the side of the bypass. The private hospital was billed Rupees 4 lakh and 96 thousand in 10 days. The cost of plaster, dressing, cotton, etc. alone is one lakh rupees. Eventually, the doctor at the hospital told him he feared he would lose his leg. Bikash decided to go to Vellore. He went to CMC for treatment after signing the bond at the hospital.

One lakh 19 thousand rupees was billed in 19 days in Vellore, said Bikash. The damaged leg also had to be removed. The commission examined the cost of Bikash's treatment at the Kolkata hospital. It is alleged that the exemption was not given as per the guidelines of the commission.

During the hearing of the case, the commission directed the accused hospital to reconsider its bill. At the same time, the bill is being sent to all the private hospitals in the state, said the chairman of the health commission. According to him, "Why do patients leave Vellore despite having good doctors and improved infrastructure in the state? Let all the private hospitals in the state look at the Vellore bill and understand where their shortcomings are and correct them accordingly. "

Some information for those who want to be treated or someone who needs treatment in Vellore.

A few words about CMC in Vellore.......

1 / Vellore: -

Can't wait to tell you how useful and advanced Vellore's treatment is. We usually go to Vellore if we can't find a way. I am trying to write about the details of how to get there, where to stay, cost, medicine, communication, and appointment so that everyone can help. The process is very systematic, just a little complicated.

2 / Language: -

If you know Hindi / English well, it shouldn't be a problem, but now 70% of the patients are Bengali (Bangladesh & West Bengal). So even if it is

Bengali, the work will go away.

3 / Appointment: -

There are basically two types of appointments

1. General appointment (see a junior doctor)

2. Private appointment (see a senior doctor)

If anyone goes from here, one must take a private appointment.

4 / Appointment Procedure: -

There are usually two types of appointments, offline and online. Since we are leaving Bengal, we have to make an online appointment assuming there is no one there. Online Appointments: - It may take you 15 days to 3 months to get a private appointment with any department in such a crowded place.

5 / Offline Appointment: -

As soon as you enter the main gate of Vellore, you will see "SILVER GATE FOR NEW APPOINTMENT". Once you report your problem there, they will make an appointment with the specified department. In this case, you are sure to get a private appointment in 3-30 days.

6 / Emergency treatment: -

There is a separate EMERGENCY section for this, go there. They will tell the whole process. General appointment: - Can be done online or offline. You will get an appointment in 1-3 days.

7 / Which department will you go to?

If you want to make an appointment online, it is important to know which department you will take it to, otherwise, it is a waste of time and money. Examples, ENT, Hormone Problems, Endocrinology, Cancer Patient: - Oncology, etc. If you do not understand, you can find out by calling the helpline provided on their site. If they say a problem, they will tell the department. You have to choose CLINIC under the department according to the symptoms of your disease.

8 / Stay: -

There are plenty of lodges here as the demand for rooms is high. You may get a double or triple bedroom from 150-200 to 1500-2000 rupees. The farther you go from CMC, the lower the lodge rate will be. About 7-8 minutes' walk away you will get a room for 200-250 rupees. You can book a room for 24 hours a day and find a good room at a lower price by searching a little.

9 / Eating: -

There are many Bengali hotels, you can get rice for 40-60 rupees/mill. You can also enjoy South Indian food, but you can not pull more than 3-4 days.

10 / CMC DETAILS: -

CMCs have main 3 to 4 buildings.

1. OPD BUILDING (outdoor patients) - You will see a doctor basically in this building. The work is usually done on the 5th floor.

> Ground floor: - This floor is allotted for all tests. Almost all tests including blood, x-ray, and urine tests are done here. You have to go to the payment cash counter with the slip that the doctor has prescribed. CASH / DEBIT-CREDIT-ATM CARD / CRISS CARD is used for payment (details are given later).

The payment slip will say where you need to go to which room. Suppose blood tests - G20, XRAY- G11 are like this. You come in the morning and stand in line and get the tests done. Work started at 6 AM. You have to stand in line from 5-5:30 to get there early.

> On the first floor, second floor, and third floor in different rooms of different departments see the private, general doctor. Your appointment letter will tell you where to go on which floor.

For example: -

> **OPD Building** SECOND FLOOR 210, report to MRO at 10:30 AM ... This means you have to go in front of room 210 on the second floor and submit the appointment copy at MRO COUNTER at 10:30 AM. Even if you retreat 1 hour ago, there is usually no problem.

> **ISSCC BUILDING**: - It is as important as OPD BUILDING. Jobs of New Appointment, Repeat Appointment, Pharmacy, Chris Card, CASH PAYMENT, etc. are done here. Of course, Doctors see the shots on the upper floor also.

11 / NEW APPOINTMENT: -

Payment for new appointments, tests, etc. is usually made in cash at the counter from 4-10 a.m.

12 / REPEAT APPOINTMENT: -

A doctor's re-appointment is made at counter 11-13. In this case, you have to tell the doctor at the counter when he wants to see you, they will give you an appointment.

Pharmacy: - Usually gives medicine to patients for 3 months. You have to stand in line to get the medicine by paying at the pharmacy.

13 / CRISS CARD: -

If you make this card, your harassment will be much less. Just show your HOSPITAL NO. (PATIENT ID) and you will get all the help regarding the Criss card from counter 402. You have to pay in advance (through cash transfer/atm transfer) on this Criss card. However, I continue to work using the ATM card. The fun of a Criss card is that you don't have to stand in a big line for payment because there is a Criss card payment counter in almost all places.

14 / APPOINTMENT DATE CHANGE: -

Forward or backward...

Give a long line at ISSCC building HELPDESK with the payment slip. It is a very crowded place and as soon as they arrange the date change then your problem will be solved there. (Only if the date is empty before)

15 / PMR BUILDING: -

Generally, it can be called the physiotherapy department. You have to go to this department for all kinds of physiotherapy equipment, shoes, duplicate breasts (silicone breasts), etc. The payment slip or appointment letter will mention PMR BUILDING.

16 / WARD BUILDING: -

Patients are admitted here as they need surgery and treatment. Such a clean and sterile place may not even be the rooms in your home. To emphasize DIAGNOSIS they give a lot of tests. Then he treats only when the disease is caught. (Here it is ahead of Kolkata).

Test shots are basically done in 3 places.

17 / OPD BUILDING: -

Usually, the maximum persons' test is done here. However, for some special tests like USG, it may take 3-4 days. So when you talk to the doctor, request him to send your tests to ALPHA Clinic. If they prick with a pen, your 3-4 day job will be done in 1 day.

18 / EMERGENCY PATIENT: -

There is an emergency test system for this. You will not receive any report of these tests. This will go to the doctor directly who sees you. So, there is no problem. I heard that you have to apply differently to get the report.

THE MAIN HOSPITAL CAMPUS:

In accordance with the vision of the founder, CMC has, through the last many decades, through sheer hard work, prayer, and dedication evolved into one of the pioneering institutions in specialized medical care rendering invaluable service to a large number of patients from every state in India and neighboring countries in the spirit of Jesus Christ.

CMC located on Ida Scudder Road, in the heart of Vellore town, is a large 2210 (average bed) hospital with 144 specialized departments/units. The various consultants and the days they conduct outpatient clinics are listed below.

Being a referral hospital CMC is in a position to provide specialized medical care to patients requiring treatment in more than one area/ailment/disease. This is due to the unique availability of all the specialized departments/units under one roof and due to the existence of close understanding and harmony amongst these departments.

Moreover, CMC has a system by which it gives exposure to all consultants by periodically sending them to various national/international conferences, symposiums, and specialized training overseas to acquire the latest knowledge and skills in their respective areas so that they can provide high-quality medical service to all patients coming to the institution.

ISSCC FOR WOMEN & CHILDREN

The Ida S.Scudder Centenary Center for Women and Children houses the departments of Obstetrics & Gynaecology, Reproductive Medicine,

Child Health, Neonatology, Paediatric Surgery, and Developmental Paediatrics. There are 424 beds for in-patient care in this facility.

PERIPHERAL FACILITIES

In addition to the main campus on Ida Scudder Road, there are a number of peripheral facilities which are also departments of CMC.

OPHTHALMOLOGY DEPARTMENT

The Department of Ophthalmology at the Christian Medical College is located in the Schell campus 2 km away from the main campus, on Arni Road, Vellore. It is a 100-bedded tertiary eye care center offering "state of the art" comprehensive and specialty eye care including outreach (camp) facilities.

The services offered are-

- Cataract surgery- manual and phacoemulsification surgery with the latest microscopes, phacoemulsification machines, and premium intraocular lenses.
- Cornea and ocular surface disorders- including corneal transplants, contact lenses, and keratoconus treatment.
- Glaucoma services- glaucoma diagnoses and treatment including lasers, filtering surgeries, and drainage devices.
- Orbit and oculoplastic services- management of thyroid eye disease, ocular plastics, and facial aesthetics.
- Pediatric ophthalmology- Management of pediatric cataracts, CVI management, ROP screening.
- Ocular oncology- Management of tumors of the eye such as retinoblastoma, choroidal melanoma, and lid tumors.
- Retina and vitreous- medical and surgical management of various types of retinal diseases such as retinal detachment, and diabetic retinopathy. A facility for retinal lasers is also available.
- Squint- diagnosis and treatment of squint and amblyopia
- Uvea- diagnosis, and management of uveitis and inter-department collaboration with various other departments such as rheumatology.
- Emergency services- 24-hour emergency and trauma management with all the necessary equipment required for surgery of ocular trauma.
- Low vision services- diagnosis and management of the low vision and community-based rehabilitation including help for procuring blindness certificates for residents of Vellore.

The hospital is a 3-story building with outpatient departments, examination rooms, laser rooms, all necessary investigative equipment, optical dispensary, laboratory, pharmacy, inpatient facility, and theatre all under one roof. In addition, there are car parking and canteen facilities.

Patients with eye problems should go directly to this department for registration, investigations, and treatment. In order to reach the Ophthalmology Department, one can take an auto-rickshaw or local town bus Route No.2 from the main CMC bus stop or Route No.1 from Bagayam, near CHAD Hospital, and ask to be dropped off at Eye Hospital.

Patients can make appointments by advance booking by coming to the hospital registration counter. In addition, patients with existing Schell hospital numbers can avail the online appointment system through the CMC appointment portal available on the internet. The OPD functions from Monday to Friday as full working days, Saturday as a half working day, and is closed on Sundays.

For further details please contact the Main Reception or write to the Head, Ophthalmology Department, Schell Campus, Arni Road, Vellore - 632 001, Tamil Nadu. Suggestions for improvement or complaints can also be made to the head of the department.

Tel number- 0416 228- 1201, 0418228- 1309.

MENTAL HEALTH CENTRE (MHC)

CMC's Department of Psychiatry is situated on the Christian Medical College Campus at Bagayam, 7km south of the main campus. Patients (infants, children, adolescents, and adults) with psychiatric problems and neuro-psychological disabilities may go directly to this department for registration, evaluation, and treatment. Both inpatient and outpatient services are available.

For further details please contact the Head of the Department of Psychiatry, Mental Health Centre, Christian Medical College, Bagayam, and Vellore-632 002. E-mail: childpsych@cmcvellore.ac.in. Phone No.0416-2284307.

In order to reach the Mental Health Centre (MHC), take No.1 or 2 town bus from the bus stop near the CMC out-gate which goes to Bagayam. If traveling by personal or hired transport asks for directions to the Bagayam Police station. The Main gate to MHC is next to the Bagayam Police Station.

NAMBIKKAI NILAYAM

Nambikkai Nilayam is a facility for children with Neurodevelopmental Disorders, under the Child and Adolescent Psychiatry Unit, Department of Psychiatry. The facility was initially established in 1978 for children with intellectual disabilities but subsequently started treating children with various neurodevelopmental disorders like Intellectual Disability, Developmental Delays, Autism, Language Disorders, and Specific Learning Disabilities.

The emphasis of treatment is on caring for these children by involving the parents and family members through education and therapeutic involvement. The services are provided with input from members of a multidisciplinary team of experienced Psychiatrists, Clinical Psychologists, Rehabilitation Psychologists, Occupational therapists, Speech therapists, Special Educators, and nurses. Based on the child's cognitive, communicative, and adaptive functions, outpatient follow-up and/or a 12-week parent training intervention as daycare or inpatient is provided in either of the following therapy programs: Infant Stimulation, Autism therapy, Early Intervention, and Advanced Intervention.

For further details please contact:

Child and Adolescent Psychiatry, Department of Psychiatry (Mental Health Centre), Christian Medical College, Bagayam, Vellore-632002.E-mail: childpsych@cmcvellore.ac.in. Phone No.0416-2284307.

REHABILITATION INSTITUTE

The Rehabilitation Institute is an inpatient facility under the Department of Physical Medicine and Rehabilitation (PMR) and was dedicated in 1966 by the then Union Minister for Health Dr.Sushila Nayyar. This service has expanded in the year 2018 to 100 bedded inpatient facilities.

This institute offers comprehensive multidisciplinary rehabilitation for people with spinal cord injuries, acquired brain injuries, cerebral palsy, and other conditions leading to cognitive and physical disabilities and amputees. The multidisciplinary team comprises physiatrists, specially trained nurses, physiotherapists, occupational therapists, speech therapists, prosthetists and orthotics, social workers, psychologists, and rehab engineers.

Movement analysis lab, Urodynamics Lab, Diagnostic and Therapeutic Ultrasound services. Electromyography services Spinal cord regeneration research laboratory and multi-terrain wheelchair training are few of the research come service facilities available. Rehab Research Laboratory has also been set up to focus on Rehabilitation Engineering to develop innovative technology for people with disabilities. There is also a canteen and kitchen service for the in-patients. Rehabilitated severely disabled persons are encouraged to join in a suitable vocation and, we offer vocational training for the needy people along with free food and accommodation through MVT Home located near Rehabilitation Institute, Bagayam.

For further details, visit this link:

https://www.cmch-vellore.edu/Departments.aspx?depttype=ALL

In order to reach the Rehabilitation Institute, take No.1 or 2 town bus from the bus stop near the CMC outgate which goes to Bagayam.

Chittoor Campus, Christian Medical College Vellore

The Chittoor Campus of the Christian Medical College Vellore has made major strides in terms of its development over the last couple of years. The infrastructure for a 130- bedded hospital has been put in place and this hospital is currently active. The campus has four state-of-the-art operation theatres, which have been fully operational since September 2016. The fittings inclusive of surgical and anesthesia machines involve the latest technology. A total of 3000 surgeries have been performed during this per neighboring.

The patients on whom surgeries were performed include those from the Chittoor district, the surrounding states (from where a large proportion of the patients come) as well as those from the countries. The surgeries involve several departments including General Surgery, Paediatric Surgery, Orthopaedics, Orthopaedic Oncology, Spine, Dental Surgery, Endocrine Surgery, Obstetrics & Gynaecology, and several other specialties with excellent anesthetic facilities.

A total of more than 11,000 outpatients are seen per month. The patient load comprises all specialties including Internal Medicine, General Surgery, Paediatrics, Psychiatry, Anaesthesia, Orthopaedics, ENT, Ophthalmology, Endocrinology, Cardiology, and Community Health. The hospital has a state-of-the-art laboratory that is well-equipped with the latest technologies. The emergency services have facilities for non-invasive ventilation, which are performed very frequently. The prosthetic and orthotic manufacturing units have been established, the only one of their kind in southern Andhra Pradesh.

HOW TO REACH VELLORE AND CMC (Main Campus)

CMC is located at Vellore, the district headquarters of Vellore District, Tamil Nadu. The main campus is situated on Ida Scudder Road about 2 km from the main bus stand. Those coming to Vellore by broad gauge train should get off at Katpadi Junction. The main campus is about 6 km from Katpadi Junction.

Town buses (No.1 & 2) operate regular day and night service from Katpadi railway station via CMC to Bagayam. Taxis and auto-rickshaws are always available at Katpadi Railway station and will charge approximately Rs.400/- for taxis and Rs.170/-for auto-rickshaws to bring you to the main campus.

You can approach the Emergency center for emergency Medical care at the entrance of the Katpadi Railway station.

Patients traveling to Vellore by meter gauge train (Villupuram-Tirupathi line) should get off at Vellore cantonment station which is 2 k.m from the main campus.

Auto-rickshaws and cycle-rickshaws are available at approximately Rs.100/- and Rs.70/- respectively to take you to the main campus. Patients who arrive at Chennai and wish to come by bus to Vellore should take bus no.102 from the new bus stand in Koyambedu. This service is available every 15 to 20 minutes and is about a 3-hour journey, a distance of 140 k.m.

For those coming by air, the options available are either to come into Chennai city from the airport (by bus, taxi, or suburban train) and find a suitable connecting train from Chennai Central to Katpadi or a bus from Koyembedu or take a taxi right from the airport to CMC, the main campus at an approximate cost of Rs.3500/-.

OUTPATIENT DEPARTMENT (O.P.D) BUILDING OUT PATIENTS SERVICES

The Out-Patient block is a four-storeyed building situated on your right as you enter the main gate. Most of the Out-Patient clinics function in this building. The OutPatient Services department is a very busy area treating more than 7,500 patients per day.

Receptions:

• Reception staff at the OPD and Centenary building will assist patients with information and accompany them, if need be, and provide any sort of procedural assistance if patients may require it. Please contact G-12 (OPD Reception) for assistance.

• The Main Reception is located in the Main Building near the Chapel; the staff there will assist and provide information to In-patients, Out-patients, patient relatives, visitors, students, and staff.

OPD Entrance Gates:

Entrance checks and instructions:-

• At the entrance gates patients should produce the appointment slip and the Hospital Number card for verification by the security staff.

• After successful verification the patient and one relative will each be given one wrist band which is like a pass to enter the OPD building.

• Only one relative of a patient is allowed to enter the OPD building.

• The patient and relative can enter the OPD building only 30 minutes before the appointment time mentioned in the appointment slip.

• Large suitcases and luggage bags are not permitted inside the OPD building; patients are requested to leave the luggage in their lodges.

<u>REGISTRATION PROCEDURES</u>

The registration procedure in CMC allows patients to register themselves as General patient or Private Patient.

i) New General Registration (This facility is for general patients who come to CMC without a prior online appointment).

a) Fill in the registration forms kept at the ISSCC Reception No.401. Please fill all details accurately according to your Government photo I.D as they are permanent records that you may require later for reimbursement or further correspondence. If you know the area Pin Code, enter it correctly on the registration form. Please give your present active mobile number or email.

b) After filling the form, proceed to the ISSCC building adjacent to the OPD building for triaging (counter No.401).

c) After triaging proceed to the cash counters (MCTT) and submit the filled-in registration forms with registration fees of Rs.250/- for General patients.

d) Hospital Number Card:

• Hospital Number card is provided to every new General patient which serves as a patient number card.

• This card is mandatory at the entry gates and for all services within the hospital premises.

• Fresh Hospital Number Card will be issued in replacement of lost/damaged card for a fee of Rs.100/- after verification.

• New private patient registration

• Repeat patient appointments for revisits.

• Against cancellation appointments (Tatkal appointments)

• Cash counter for investigations and appointments.

e) Proceed to the appropriate clinic with the payment receipt. This receipt will have your name, hospital number, date, reporting time, and location of the clinic. Kindly check the name, hospital number, date, and time of appointment.

f) Submit the payment receipt to the Medical Record Officer at the clinic you are visiting. It is important that the Hospital Number Card / Patient Number Card be kept safe. Please visit the OP clinic at the specified time on your registration slip.

g) Please report half an hour before your appointment time.

h) Kindly bring your photo I.D issued by Government (Aadhar Card, Pan Card or driving license, Passport) when you visit OPD

.

ii)NEW PRIVATE REGISTRATION

PRIVATE PATIENT FACILITY CENTRE (PPFC) at Silvergate 600 (This facility is for private patients and repeat private patients).

Note: Don't fill out the registration form for revisits.

<u>Caution :</u>

-- Kindly do not seek middlemen like brokers or agents for early/tatkal appointments.

-- As they are provided for free by CMC.

-- Patients should visit the PPFC in Silver Gate 600 in person for early appointments.

A yearly check-up could save your life.

<u>Online Pre-registration process :</u>

New Private patients should do registration online. www.cmch-vellore.edu --> Are you --> a patient? --> Patient Portal --> Proceed. After successful online registration, you will get a User ID

• Please note down the user ID and password, which should

be presented adjacent to the Silver Gate for triage and appointment.

• If you know which department to go to/ you have a referral letter please inform the staff at the Reception.

• Your token number and triage station will be displayed on the television in front of you in the waiting area.

• After triage proceeds for payment.

• If you have urgency for an appointment please explain that to the triage staff who will help you.

• Please note that online Pre-registration can be done from your smartphone, personal computer, or the registration room adjacent to the Silver Gate (New Private Patient Facility).

• Every private patient will be given a Hospital Number Card.

• Your repeat appointments can be made using OPAD, Credit / Debit cards at Silver Gate.

• Please ensure that you have deposited or topped up Out Patient Advance (OPAD) before seeing the consultant. OPAD deposits can be done at any cash counter, refer to page 24 for OPD instructions.

Advantage of Pre-Registration

Patients who have already done Pre-registration online can skip the queue for the pre-registration procedure near Silver Gate.

REVISITS

• General patients must pay Rs.130/- for a re-visit towards repeat registration charges and private patients must pay Rs.320/- for a revisit.

• Private Patients who have paid the consultation fees of Rs.900/- need to pay Rs.750/- only as consultation repeat - cum registration fees for re-visit after three months.

• Kindly produce your Hospital Number card, don't fill out the registration form again.

• Patients with OPAD/ Credit / Debit cards can pay on their respective OP Floors.

• For cash payments please use the cash counters on the OPD Ground floor and ISSCC Building Ground Floor.

Online Appointments CMC Mobile App

Appointments can also be booked through CMC Mobile App. Mobile App named CMC Patient Portal can be downloaded from the CMC website and Google play store.

Online Appointments (advance booking)

Online appointments can be booked in advance on our website www.cmch-vellore.edu --> Are you --> a patient? --> Patient Portal --> Proceed and follow the instructions.

If you have any queries, please go through the FAQs (Frequently Asked Questions) on the website.

-- New and repeat OP appointments can be made online for General and private patients (Indian and International Patients).

-- Date change is allowed online five times on the CMC website only for the appointments booked during the COVID 19 pandemic. Change in appointment date will be allowed only up to one day before the day of the Appointment date.

-- Appointments booked online cannot be refunded or canceled.

Against Cancellation of Appointments (Silver Gate 600 ISSCC Building, Ground Floor, Counter No.492)

• If you are a New or Repeat patient (with Hosp.No.) and you don't get an early appointment, please contact Silver Gate 600 / 492 counters for assistance.

• Patients with inter-departmental referrals (general) will be given priority. Private interdepartmental referrals can go to Silver Gate (600) Monday - Saturday between 1. p.m to 6. p.m for appointments.

• Please bring a valid Government-issued photo ID proof along with the patient for early date change at this counter.

• If your patient is very sick please approach the ISSCC building Reception/OPD Reception for urgent help.

• No extra charges are levied for appointments. Do not pay money to middlemen to get appointments.

Payment counters

For patient convenience and quick transactions, all floors at OPD block are cash and card counters. Patients are requested to use OPAD, Credit/ Debit card, cash, or online payments (in Mobile App/ CMC Website) for payments of investigations and appointments.

REFUNDS for appointments:

1. No refund for General new and general repeat registrations.

2. No refund for Private repeat registration of Rs.320/-.

3. No refund after date change.

4. Refund for private new registration (Rs.900/-) and three-month renewal (Rs.750/-) is refundable one day before the date of appointment after deducting the registration fee of Rs.320/-.

5. Date change is possible only one day before the date of appointment.

6. You can contact the OPD Supervisors at Counter No.G31/G32, ISSCC ground floor for assistance with refunds.

Unit changes are done through the Medical Superintendent's Office. Patients doing online registration can send an email to msoffice@cmcvellore.ac.in with the reason for the change.

Refund Timings:

24 hours at room No.105, first floor of the Main building.

OPAD (Outpatient Advance)

OPAD is an Advance Payment for your Out Patient expenses)

Advantages of OPAD

--Easy and quick transaction.

-- Need not carry a large sum of money in hand all the time.

-- Quick, easy and simple refund of the remaining money.

-- Can avoid long queues.

-- You can top up your OPAD at any one of the payment counters.

Minimum Deposit--Rs.2, 000/-In multiples of--Rs.1,000/- Maximum Limit -- Rs.20,000/-

— OPAD refund up to Rs.2, 000/- is available at any one of the cash counters with your original cash receipt and ID proof.

— Above Rs.2,000/- can be refunded at Billing Section (Room No.105) with your original cash receipt and ID Proof.

<u>REGISTRATION TIMINGS:</u>

Monday-Friday 6.30 AM - 11.00 AM (Morning OP) and 6.30 AM - 3.00 PM (Afternoon OP)

Saturday 6.30 AM - 11.00 AM

<u>Medical Records Officer</u>

Each clinic has a Medical Records Officer who is responsible for the functioning of the clinic from patient registration to managing patient records.

<u>Floor Manager</u>

Every floor has a Floor Manager. You can contact them if you need any help or if you have any suggestions or encounter problems during your treatment at the hospital. Following are the phone numbers:

OPD Building –

1st Floor — 8300205228

2nd Floor — 8300205229

3rd Floor — 8300205486

Ground Floor — 8300205302

Basement — 8300205227

ISSCC Building — 8300205230

<u>CMC Tele-consultation</u>

The Tele-Consultation facility has been functioning in CMC since 8th April 2020. During the COVID 19 Lockdown, the Tele- Consultation facility is a big boon and advantage for patients who could not travel to CMC Vellore. Repeat patients and new patients can book Tele Consultation appointments on the CMC Website.

The procedure to book a Tele-Consultation appointment in CMC, Vellore for new and repeat patients is as follows:

1. Visit the CMC website www.cmch-vellore.edu — > Are you?

— > Patient? — > Patient Portal — > Login using Hospital Number and Password and select 'Tele Consultation'.

2. Select the required Department and Doctor and proceed for payment online:

-- Rs.900/- for the first visit

-- Rs. 750/- for the first visit to other departments and repeat registration once in 3 months.

-- Rs.330/- repeat registration within 3 months.

3. After the appointment is fixed, you will receive instructions| and a call from CMC on the day of the appointment.

4. After consultation, prescription and medical report will be sent to the patient's registered email I.D.

Shalom Family Medicine Centre at CDC

The Shalom Family Medicine center at CDC, Sathuvachari brings the services of CMC exclusively to the people of Vellore. It functions under the department of Family Medicine and is aimed to bring back the concept of a family doctor for every family. Doctors trained in the specialty of family medicine will provide comprehensive care for 90% of the health issues of all the members of a family along with referral to other specialists and coordination of care when required.

The services will include the management of common health problems for all age groups from newborn children to the elderly.

It has a blood collection area for sending samples to the main hospital lab, a pharmacy, and a treatment room for minor procedures, dressings, and ECGs.

With electronic medical records, the doctors in the center have access to all the records of the patients in the main hospital and the records of patients made in the center will also be available for the doctors in the main hospital when needed. With its focus on patient-centered medicine and continuity of care center is your point of care for all the members of your family with your personal family physician. It will function from 8 AM to 3 PM from Monday to Friday.

CMC Trauma Care Centre and Temporary COVID Health Care at Kannigapuram

CMC Vellore is currently in the process of establishing a new hospital campus in Kannigapuram, Tamil Nadu which is nearing completion. The Kannigapuram campus located in the new District of Ranipet has inaugurated its 400-bed facility for COVID -19 patients care on 17th June 2020.

The new hospital campus will be the first of its kind in southern India with more than 1000 beds and a Level 1 Trauma Care Centre. With the onset of the coronavirus pandemic, the need of the hour has led to the creation of a COVID-19 patient care facility which will be developed in three phases.

This facility would treat COVID-19-positive patients. The facility will be staffed with an expert medical team along with basic laboratory and radiological diagnostic facilities.

The patients will be assessed regularly and referred to the CMC Main hospital if requiring further management. This temporary COVID health center would predominantly cater to the Ranipet district and would act as a surge capacity for the Main Hospital also.

SILVER GATE (600) is open on Sundays for both New and Repeat registration from 7.00 a.m to 3.00 p.m.

GENERAL INSTRUCTION FOR OUR HOSPITAL AS PER FRRO ADVICE, VELLORE

1. All Foreign patients & attendants should come with Original passports and valid medical visas and attendants' visas.

2. Those that have a special endorsement in visa except Bangladesh nationalize. "Registration required" must register in FRRO online within 14 days of arrival in India" (FRRO registration).

3. Those who have more than 180 days of valid Visa must also register in FRRO (within 14 days of arrival) online. (Types of visa- Med, Medx, Med-1, Med -2, and X -misc).

4. Foreign nationals coming for medical treatment will have to come on a medical visa preferably, but any category of visa is accepted for both Outpatient and Inpatient Treatment.

5. Treatment for diseases that require organ transplants will be permitted only on a medical visa.

6. Medical visa is mandatory for Pakistani Nationals requiring indoor medical treatment.

7. Hospital has to mandatorily comply with C-Form formalities within 24 hours of inpatient admission.

8. In the event of a patient attendant falling sick, requiring inpatient medical treatment/ outpatient treatment can be rendered on the same visa.

Book through the IRO online facility (web i.d and steps below)

Step 1: Web I.D: http://www.cmch-vellore.edu

Step 2: Patient Service

Step 3: Appointments

Step 4: For foreign nationals, please "click here" to book through the IPO online facility.

All days 24 hrs

(b) PHYSICAL MEDICINE AND REHABILITATION COUNTER

Monday to Friday: 8.00 a.m. to 4.30 p.m.

Saturday: 8.00 a.m. to 11.45 noons

(c) AK LAB COUNTERS: 8.00 a.m to 4.30 p.m

(d) B-WARD COUNTER: 10.00 a.m. to 6.30 p.m.

In the OPD Building, each floor has two cash counters. You can use your cash, OPAD / Debit/ Credit card to do payments at these counters.

(e) OPAD Advance counter 212 (OPD building 2nd floor)

OPAD/ Credit/ Debit cards are accepted.

PROCEDURE FOR PAYMENT OF BILLS

Cash should be paid at cash counters only. Demand drafts are accepted at all cash counters. Payments can be made through OPAD/ Debit/ Credit cards on all floors, in ISSCC Building (4 to 14 Counters and in OPD Building (7 to 10, 10a, 10b counters).

Very poor patients who cannot afford to pay the registration fees of Rs.250/- or revisit fees of Rs.130/- are requested to approach the OPD Reception (G12) for free registration.

To avoid over-crowding in the clinics only one relative will be permitted to accompany a patient.

Entry and Exit points:

Gate 1: Entry for patients who have Doctor's appointments on the same day.

Gate 2: Only exit.

Gate 3: Entry for patients who have blood investigations ECG.

Gate 4: Entry for patients who have to go for x-rays and to P.C.F.

Note: Kindly produce your Hospital Number Card at all the entry-level.

GENERAL PATIENT/ PRIVATE PATIENT

If you choose to be a General Patient, you will be seen by one of the doctors in the appropriate clinic. But if there are concerns a second opinion is always asked for from a consultant at no extra cost.

If you are a Private Patient, you will meet the consultant in the appropriate outpatient clinic or by prior appointment at other times. In some specialty clinics during the first visit, you will be seen by a junior Consultant / Registrar and on the second visit by the Consultant. All fees and charges collected go to the institutional funds and no doctor working in CMC have any private practice. When you (as a general patient or private patient) are referred to another department for an opinion or treatment, the option is available to you to be seen as a general patient or as a private patient.

Interdepartmental Referrals:

Referral Consultation on the same day to a different department for a private consultation is Rs. 750.00 Registration charges for a consultant in the same unit are also Rs.750.00. Please show your Hospital card / OPAD at all service stations. Private interdepartmental referrals can be done in the Silver Gate (Private Patient Facility)

Timings: Mon - Fri: 12 Noon - 9 p.m. Saturday: 12 Noon - 6 p.m. Sunday : 12 Noon - 3 p.m.

ACCESS - 603

(Access to Corporate Cashless Entry and Services) ACCESS is a single-window facility for processing Cashless requests.

All patients referred by companies should first go to the ACCESS Counter (603) adjacent to New Silver Gate with the company referral letter to get their paper processed.

New Company referred patients can book an advance appointment by sending an email to access@cmcvellore.ac.in with the company referral letter, investigation reports, and the below-mentioned details:

-- Patient Name

--Age, DOB

--Sex

--Marital Status

--Required Appointment Date & Department

--Mobile Number

Repeat company referred patients can book appointments online if there is a credit validity date. Repeat patients who don't have credit validity dates can book an appointment by sending an email to access@cmcvellore.ac.in with the old referral letter mentioning the Hospital Number, Department, and the date of appointment required.

Procedure to book repeat appointment:

Go to the website www.cmch-vellore.edu --> Are you --> a patient? --> Patient Portal and follow the instructions. Insurance patients who need to avail of cashless facilities for inpatient must inform the treating doctor. For cashless registration contact

ACCESS (603) with the following documents:
* Photocopy of patient's Health Card
* Photocopy of patients ID Proof (anyone)
(Voter's Card, PAN card, Driving License, Passport, or Aadhar Card)
* Photocopy of Employee ID Card in case of Corporate Insurance
* Outside Hospital Reports if any
Contact Number: 0416 - 2283604/ 6193
Email: access@cmcvellore.ac.in

<u>ALPHA CLINIC</u>

(1) Any private patient who wants to be seen quickly can approach this facility.

(2) You can request your consultant that you be seen in ALPHA Clinic. Call the ALPHA Clinic reception and request an appointment to be seen by a particular consultant. (Ph.No. 0416- 2282299).

(3) You may request for a particular consultant to see you. However, if he/ she is busy, he/ she has a right to decline. The Patient Service Manager can help you find a suitable doctor for consultation in his/ her absence.

(4) If your consultant is happy to see you in ALPHA Clinic on a non-OP day, you can be seen in ALPHA Clinic by paying the difference in consultation fees.

(5) Consultation fee for the first visit is Rs.1, 765/- (including free second visit within a week and medical report).

(6) Consultation fee for a repeat visit within 3 months is Rs.380/- per visit.

(7) Consultation fee for a repeat visit after 3 months is Rs.1, 475/-.

(8) We encourage the use of Patient Identification cards/credit/debit cards as ALPHA Clinic is run in a cashless format.

(9) You can do a Master's Health check at ALPHA Clinic. The charges for such a check-up are available with the Patient Service Manager in ALPHA Clinic.

(10) Advance booking is not allowed in ALPHA Clinic. Appointments are done one day in advance.

(11) Same-day booking can be done through the Patient Service Manager if a consulting slot and the consultant is available.

(12) If the consultant does not see you, your cash will be refunded as per CMC policy.

(13) Your appointment slot will be open for 3 hours pending payment. If payment has not been made within 3 hours, the appointment slot will be

canceled automatically.

(14) For problem/query you can contact the Patient Service Manager in ALPHA Clinic, Ph: 0416 -2282299.

Due to Covid, as a decongestion activity for OPD, the Alpha Clinic services are stopped and normal private OPD is functioning in the ALPHA clinic.

<u>EMERGENCIES</u>

(A) Accident & Emergency Medicine

The Accident & Emergency Department is open 24 hours for acutely ill patients who arrive at CMC after regular clinic hours needing immediate care. The triage nurse will assess the patient and issue permission slips for registration.

ALL PATIENTS MUST REGISTER AT THE CASUALTY COUNTER PAYING Rs.320/-.Counters are available to pay for emergency investigations and drugs at the Emergency Department.

(B) Paediatric Casualty

The Paediatric Casualty department in the ISSCC is open 24 hours and treats children who are brought after regular clinic hours and require immediate care. THEY SHOULD REGISTER AT THE CASUALTY COUNTER OR COUNTER NO.15 in ISSCC Building paying Rs.320/- after getting a permission slip from Paediatric Casualty.

Counter No.15 in ISSCC is open for registration up to 12.00 midnight. Thereafter registration can be made at counter No.3 next to the Accident & Emergency Department.

(C) CHEST PAIN UNIT

Patients with chest pain should go directly to this Unit, situated at the entrance of the main campus.

<u>ESTIMATION OF COST</u>

If you would like to know the approximate cost of your treatment writes directly to the Head of the concerned department or unit. It is advisable to estimate your total cost before coming here. The expenses will possibly include charges for such items as registration, revisits, tests, investigations, medicine, diet, theatre, anesthesia, blood, oxygen, bed and nursing, radiation therapy, physiotherapy, and occupational therapy, whenever these are advised by the doctor.

Your total cost will depend on the choices you make, whether you wish to be seen as a general patient or a private patient; or whether you choose a private, semi-private or general bed as an in-patient.

Patients who require open-heart surgery, kidney transplant, dialysis, and other highly specialized procedures, should obtain an estimated cost of such procedures from their doctors before arriving at Vellore. Such patients should generate funds from their own contacts. However, some economically backward patients have been able to collect money from sources like Prime Minister's relief fund, Chief Minister's relief fund, various charity organizations, and appeals in newspapers for expensive treatment.

Another important factor that will affect the total cost is the length of admission which is determined by your illness and the subsequent treatment. Though doctors will give you information as to the approximate duration of hospitalization, it is sometimes difficult to give an accurate estimation as it will, depending primarily on your condition, the number of investigations and consultations required before treatment, and how well you respond to the treatment given.

Apart from the above, there will be other costs incurred such as boarding and lodging. It is wise to budget for all the above and to provide for sufficient reserve. It is important to keep in mind that specialized treatment is expensive and takes time.

<u>**REFERRALS**</u>

If you are referred to another department for opinion/ treatment, the option is available to you to be seen either as a General or Private patient. If you choose to be a General patient and the clinic you are referred to is on the same day, contact the MRO of that clinic for an appointment.

However, if the clinic you are referred to is on another day, you have to pay Rs.130/- for a General patient at payment counters showing the referral slip. If you do not show the referral slip your chart will be sent to your previous clinic.

To see a consultant get an appointment by making a payment of Rs.750/- at Silver Gate (Private Patient Facility) Room No.600. Monday - Saturday between 1.00 PM to 6.00 p.m.

<u>**SAFETY OF YOUR REGISTRATION CARD**</u>

The registration card (Hospital Number Card) issued to you is an important document. Please retain it carefully. To obtain a duplicate registration number card contact G-31/G-32 (Supervisor counter) on the ground floor of the ISSCC building. Your Hospital number card is mandatory. Do not register for a new card as this is expensive and time-consuming for you and us.

OUT-PATIENT CLINICS

On reaching the appropriate out-patient clinic, submit the appointment slip to the MRO, please be seated in the waiting hall. When your medical chart reaches the clinic, the MRO in the hall will call your name. On producing the payment slip which you obtained during the registration, the MRO will send your chart to one of the doctors. If you have registered as a Private patient, your chart will go to a consultant or his/ her approved assistant. Your name will be called out when your turn comes and you will be seen by the doctor. Report to MRO according to your reporting time.

When you meet with your doctor feel free to discuss all your health problems with him/her, giving all relevant information about your sickness and follow the advice given. If the doctor decides to have some clinical tests done, such as an examination of blood, urine, stool, etc., you will be issued the required forms. The steps to be followed are described below under the heading "Tests and Investigations".

If the doctor decides to put you on treatment, you will be given prescription slips for the purchase of medicine/injections and/ or treatment procedures. The steps to be followed are given below. If the doctor decides to admit you as an inpatient, he/she will give you an admission order. The steps to be followed then are given below.

If the doctor decides on any other course of action, he/she will explain the details to you.

PAYMENT FOR TESTS & INVESTIGATIONS

After obtaining the lab requisition master slip from the doctor, proceed with the payment and then for the appropriate tests/ investigations.

Investigation payments can be made at all payment counters (except pharmacy counters) on the ground floor of the OPD building and ISSCC from 6.30 AM to 8.30 PM. You can pay for the next day's investigations in the evening itself. In the OPD block, each floor has a payment counter.

ONLINE PAYMENTS FOR INVESTIGATIONS/TESTS

Patients can make payments online for tests/ investigations prescribed by the doctor by visiting our website and using the following instructions.

www.cmch-vellore.edu and click Patient and Other Online Services then click Online Payments and login http:// www.cmch-vellore.edu/ Content.aspx?Pid=P160804010

Click on the test that the doctor has ordered and proceed to pay. Patients can also use CMC Mobile App for payments. You can use your Hospital Number Card which has a sufficient balance (Or Credit Card/Debit card/

net banking) to make payment and take a printout of the receipt sent to your registered email id.

Company patients

Credit patients can make payments for investigations at ACCESS (603) (Adjacent to the new Silver Gate). When ACCESS is closed payment can be made at the counters on the ground floor of the ISSCC building.

BLOOD (Location: G-20)

Counter No.G20 which is located on the Ground floor of OPD is open from 6.00 a.m. From 6.00 p.m. On Monday to Friday and on Saturdays from 7.00 a.m. to 4.00 p.m.

URINE / STOOL / SPUTUM (Location G-21)

Counter No.G21 is open from 6.00 a.m. to 6.00 p.m. from Monday to Friday. On Saturdays from 6.00 a.m to 4.00 p.m. Kindly read and follow the specific instruction before giving urine and sputum samples.

24 HOUR URINE and other routine Biochemistry samples (Location: G-21A)

Collect bottles from No.G21A on the ground floor of the O.P. building. After collecting the specimen return it to the same place.

Timings: 8.00 a.m. - 4.00 p.m. Saturday: 8.00 a.m. - 12.00 noon

X-RAYS (Location: G-11). After payment, X-rays are taken on the same OPD ground floor (G-11).

CT SCAN, MRI (Location: Radiology Dept, Main Building). After payment gets an appointment at G-11A in the OPD building and reports at instructed time.

ECG (Location: G-51)

- After payment, you will get an appointment for the procedure to be done. Report as instructed on time. For Treadmill & Holter contact 623 and for Echocardiograms contact the Cardiology Office on the ground floor of the Main building.

E.E.G., E.M.G.(Location: New lab near N2 ward main building) :

- After payment, you will get an appointment for the procedure to be done. Report as per appointment.

Gastroenterology tests (location: Second floor of OT building)

After payment, proceed to the Endoscopy room on the second floor of the Occupational Therapy Department to fix up an appointment for the prescribed tests.

Nuclear Medicine :

PET-CT Scan (Location: Adjacent to PCF, OP Block)

- After payment proceed to Nuclear Medicine Department on the first floor, opp. B ward, in the main building, and report to PCF where the test is to be done.

Pulmonary Function: (Location: ISSCC Seventh floor lift no.2)

a. Pulmonary Function Studies

(Spirometry, Lung volumes, Diffusing capacity, Bronchoprovocation, Allergen skin testing, sputum induction, Rhinomanometry, 6. min walk test.)

b. Special procedures:- Fibreoptic Bronchoscopy, Pleural Biopsy, Polysomnography, and other studies.

- Make payment at the payment counter

- Fix an appointment at Pulmonary Function Lab

- Report to the area where the test is to be done (as per instruction provided).

For conducting certain tests like cardiac catheterization angiocardiography, bronchoscopy, arthrogram, etc., and for collecting samples for certain biopsy tests, the patient has to be admitted. The concerned doctor will give admission slips in such cases.

MEDICINES AND INJECTIONS

If the doctor thinks that you need certain medicines, he will give you signed prescription forms. Take them to the Pharmacy payment counters for pricing and payment. Patients can also pay through CMC Mobile App, and through their login on the CMC Website. These counters function from 8.00 AM to 7.30 PM. The OPD Pharmacy dispensing counter will issue medicines only for the outpatients. Prescriptions of inpatients will not be processed at this counter.

If you need an injection take the procedure form given to you by your doctor and proceed to the 24-hour injection room, which is next to the post office, after payment. If you are claiming reimbursement, remember to have your receipt endorsed by the pharmacist. It is safe to buy medicines from the hospital pharmacy to ensure quality and authenticity, correct dosage, and strength of the drug. The Pharmacist will explain how to take the medication.

IMMUNIZATION FOR CHILDREN (Location: ISSCC No.450)

Children may be taken to the Immunization and Well Baby Clinic in the ISSCC straight away for immunization. After weight and temperature recording, the doctor will examine the child and give a prescription for immunizing your child. There is no need for OP registration for this.

<u>MINOR SURGERY DRESSINGS (location: OP building G-43)</u>

If you require a minor surgical procedure or dressings, you will be given a prescription for the same, specifying the charges for the treatment. Pay the amount at the payment counter after which proceeds to the O.P.Surgery dressing room (G-43) on the ground floor of the OP building.

<u>OTHER TREATMENT</u>

For all other treatments, you will be given referral slips which should be taken to the concerned doctors/ units. You will be registered and given instructions to follow.

<u>DAYCARE FACILITY</u>

For the convenience of out-patients, while they undergo specific time-consuming investigation/procedures, a daycare facility has been established at A Block / MTS-2, where patients can avail a bed and hospital diet, on payment. This facility will be available only during the period of the actual investigation/procedure done during the day i.e. between 7.00 a.m. to 7.00 a.m the following day. Patients can make a request to the doctor who will make the necessary arrangements.

The charge for the day-care facility is Rs.5, 280/- for A Block and Rs.2, 245/- for MTS-2. These charges and the fee for the investigation/ procedure should be paid and the reservation made before 3.00 p.m. the previous day. The medical chart of the patient will be sent to the ward automatically.

<u>BIRTH CERTIFICATE</u> (Location: M.S Office 2 and M.S.Office 3 main building)

For Insurance contact the Medical Superintendent's Office (No.2).

To obtain a birth certificate, death certificate, or recent corrections contact the Medical Superintendent's Office (No.3) on the main building's ground floor. A form has to be filled in and a fee of Rs.165/- for a Birth Certificate has to be paid at the payment counter in the Main building. The birth certificate can be collected in person or by post by paying Rs.220/-.

<u>MEDICAL REPORTS</u>

• To get a medical report, please request the doctor at the time of your final visit to the OPD for online payment, or he will give you a voucher for manual payment and make necessary arrangements for the medical report or guide you to the person who may be responsible to arrange this.

• After making the necessary payment, the receipt may be submitted to the secretary in the concerned department along with a self-addressed stamped envelope.

• The medical report will be posted to you later. If the report is ready before you leave you may be able to take it with you.

• Please write your hospital number and department when you correspond, in case you have not received your medical report.

IN-PATIENT SERVICES

ADMISSIONS

All admissions are made only on the advice of the doctors. If the doctor feels you require admission he/she will give you an admission slip that indicates the amount you will have to pay in advance.

The admission procedure varies slightly depending upon whether the patient seeks admission in the general ward or private ward.

All clinical departments have wards attached to them. All these wards have few semi-private rooms. At the time of admission, the patient must indicate their preference for a general, private, or semi-private room.

Inpatients Advance scheme:

The Inpatient advance scheme is an online facility for patients to pay for their advances online. Patients wanting to pay advance online can inform their doctor to prescribe their advance online, after which the patient can log in to their account using their hospital number and password as follows:

www.cmch-vellore.edu -> A Patient? -> Other Online services -

> Online payments -> Login - > Payments -> Lab order -> Select the advance amount prescribed by the doctor -> Proceed to pay online.

GENERAL WARD ADMISSIONS

i) After making the necessary payment you will have to take the admission slip to the ward and show it to the ward sister who will confirm your admission.

PRIVATE WARD ADMISSIONS

i) The private wards are A Block, 'O' block.

ii) Take your admission slip to the CBMO, No.619 on the ground floor of the main building where your admission will be confirmed after payment.

iii) At this office you will be allotted your bed as and when your turn comes. This is because there is a demand for private rooms and a waiting period of a few days or even weeks may become necessary. You are expected to keep checking with this office periodically.

iv) When your turn comes, your admission order slip will be endorsed. You should take this slip to the concerned ward where the necessary files will be prepared and you will be admitted.

MATERNITY PATIENT ADMISSIONS

i) Maternity patients in labour can go straight to the labour room in the ISSCC.

ii) They need not wait to complete admission formalities.

AT THE TIME OF ADMISSION PATIENTS MUST KEEP IN MIND THAT:

1. All admissions are made only on the advice of the doctors and not at the request of patients.

2. Routine admissions are made between 8.00 a.m. and 4.00 p.m.

3. Emergency admissions are made at all times.

4. General, semi-private and private beds/rooms are available at varying costs. For details of room/bed charges refer to page 57. It is important to note that the charge is only for the room/bed and does not include other costs which will depend on the type of bed facility available i.e. private, semi-private or general.

5. If you are claiming reimbursement of your bills, please contact Reimbursement Section 105A, Main Building, First Floor at the time of admission.

NURSING SERVICES

When you are at CMC as an in-patient, your requirements will be looked after by the Nursing Services. They will carry out the treatment planned by your doctors, make arrangements for your tests/investigations and give constant feedback to your doctor about your progress.

They will look after your convenience and comfort as a patient. You are free to contact your ward sister and seek her advice/ assistance in all matters concerning your inpatient needs.

DHOBIES AND BARBERS

Authorized dhobies and barbers can be engaged for their services on payment. The ward sister will provide you with information on this.

ATTENDANTS

It is compulsory to bring one lady attendant to stay in the ward with the patient. In private rooms, a camp cot is available for the attendant.

If a private patient does not bring a lady attendant but is in need of one he should approach the ward in charge through whom an ayah can be arranged at a nominal cost. Male attendants are permitted only during visiting hours and meal times. Patients should obtain passes (2) from the ward sister for attendants and relatives bringing food. It should be returned to the sister-in-charge on discharge. Only a lady attendant is allowed to stay with the patient during the night.

SUPPORT SERVICES FOR INPATIENT DIET

CMC has a Department of Dietetics which serves vegetarian, non-vegetarian, western, and modified diets appropriate for the health conditions of patients at the bedside of patients at meal times. Food for the attendant of the patient also can be had from the dietary. Nutritious food is prepared and served under strict standards of hygiene using modern equipment and fully competent staff.

It is not advisable to give the patient food purchased from outside since the method of preparation and the environment in which it is prepared, may not be clean and hygienic. However, cooking in the wards is strictly prohibited.

Meal Timings

For patients inwards

Breakfast - 7.00 to 8.00 a.m.

Lunch - 12.30 to 1.00 p.m.

Tea/refreshments - 3.00 to 4.00 p.m.

Dinner - 6.30 to 7.30 p.m.

Diet General Ward Private Ward Veg & Non-Veg 200.00 280.00

SPIRITUAL & PASTORAL CARE:

Spiritual and pastoral care is offered to all patients and their families by the Chaplaincy Department. It is located on the ground floor of the main building near the Chapel.

The telephone number is 0416-2282016. For further information on Chaplaincy, see page 82.

CHAPLAINCY LIBRARY

The Chaplaincy Department runs a library that is functioning in the Heritage Center located near the main entrance to the hospital. A wide range of reading materials, religious books, and magazines are available for reading. This library is open from 8:00 AM to 4.00 PM.

PROCURING MEDICINE FOR PATIENTS

General Ward Patients:

1) The medicines your doctor prescribes will be written on a prescription that will be given to you.

2) You should take the prescription to the appropriate pharmacy counter (location and timings of the pharmacy counters are listed on pages 87-90 for payment.)

3) After payment collect your medicines from the pharmacy.

Private Ward Patients:

All medicines will be automatically procured by the nurses and the cost added to the hospital bill.

INFORMATION REGARDING THE PATIENT'S PROGRESS

The patient and relatives should feel free to contact their doctor for information concerning the patient's progress.

VISITING HOURS

Week days-4.30 p.m.to 6.00 p.m. Weekends-Saturdays 3.30 p.m. to 6.00 p.m.Sundays10.00a.m. to11.30 a.m. and 3.30 p.m.to 6.30 p.m.